17 Runs

The Unbeaten Path to Unlock Life's True Potential

Garnet Morris
& Olivia Chadwick

LEGACY
launch pad
PUBLISHING

ISBN: 978-1-964377-42-1 (ebook)

ISBN: 978-1-964377-40-7 (paperback)

ISBN: 978-1-964377-41-4 (hardcover)

ISBN: 978-1-964377-43-8 (audiobook)

For more information about 17Runs and to learn how you forge your own unbeaten path, please scan the QR code below:

"*The point appears to be not just to stay the same your whole life but to grow, to really grow and open, grow in seeing, grow in awareness.*"

—Paula D'Arcy

Advance Praise for 17 Runs

"Through inspiring stories and actionable exercises, *17 Runs* challenges readers to embrace discomfort, cultivate resilience, and unlock their unique potential. A powerful guide to overcoming limiting beliefs, building good habits, and living with purpose."

—Dr. Bal Pawa, author of *The Mind-Body Cure* and co-founder of Westcoast Women's Clinic

"What does it take to face your biggest fears head-on, challenge the beliefs that are holding you back, and find the guts to keep moving forward? Read *17 Runs* by Garnet Morris and Olivia Chadwick to find out. Through raw, inspiring stories and practical exercises, this book will change your life."

—Joe Polish, founder of Genius Network and Genius Recovery

"*17 Runs* is a luminous and transformative journey of self-discovery. Morris's raw, unfiltered honesty and Chadwick's warmth and clarity are sure to stay with readers long after the final page."

—Teri Cochrane, Nutritional Counselor and Integrative Practitioner, author of the Amazon bestseller *The Wildatarian Diet: Living As Nature Intended*

"Packed with insights on habits, dreams, values, and the importance of chosen family, *17 Runs* is a guide to purpose-driven personal transformation. Through powerful storytelling, Morris and Chadwick share profound lessons on breaking free from limiting beliefs and living with integrity."

—Derek Norsworthy, entrepreneur

"Garnet Morris and Olivia Chadwick exemplify grit, determination, and emotional courage, and their book contains actionable steps to implement their lessons in your own life. A powerful reminder of the resilience of the human spirit, *17 Runs* is more than just a compelling read; it's a guide to transformation."

—Rich Christiansen, *Wall Street Journal* bestselling author, entrepreneur, and humanitarian

"*17 Runs* reinforced my commitment to personal growth and opened the door to meaningful conversations with my teenagers about overcoming challenges and shaping their own futures. I wish I could've read it when I was 13."

—Jeremy Stich MD, physician and entrepreneur

"*17 Runs* illustrates the key factors everyone needs to drive themselves forward and harness their potential to realize—and then become—the best versions of themselves."

—Taiki Shickele, research assistant, Department of Physics and Astronomy, University of British Columbia

"In *17 Runs*, Chadwick and Morris weave an engaging narrative out of rising above their circumstances, transforming their daydreams into tangible achievements, and finding a chosen family. It is an unapologetic call to readers to step boldly into their full potential."

—Tim Christiansen, founder of Adventure Yeti Marketing, partner of Classy Kin—Family Legacy Branding & Apparel

"*17 Runs* teaches why setbacks are our greatest teachers on the path to extraordinary achievement. This isn't just a guide—it's a masterclass in breaking through every obstacle to unleash your boldest dreams."

—Dorine Rivers, PhD, serial entrepreneur and author of *Brain to Bank: How to Get Your Idea Out of Your Head and Cash In*

"Chadwick's stories are well-crafted and captivating, perfectly capturing the truth and wisdom of Morris's insights. I've read thousands of business and self-help books, and *17 Runs* is in my top 10."

—Matt Nealand, B.S., EMT-LP, EMS Program Director, EMTS Academy and St. David's Round Rock, Medical Center Paramedic Program Consortium

This book is dedicated to Keenan the Magnificent and to all the Keenans in the world who have faced life's challenges early on. May this book be a tribute to your incredible inner strength and a source of support as you continue to rise above adversity. We are endlessly proud of you, and we hope this serves as a reminder of just how powerful and resilient you are.

Contents

Foreword

When Garnet first approached me about writing this book, we were in Vancouver, walking with a large group from our hotel to a local Italian restaurant, which had incredible reviews. We were all there to meet with Rich Christiansen, founder of Legado Family, who specializes in creating family bonding experiences. We were exploring the concept of "chosen family," a term we didn't yet know but which would emerge during the creation of this book.

As is often the case with large groups walking through a busy city, we naturally split into smaller factions of twos and threes, formed by unfinished conversations, walking pace, or the desire to connect with someone new. These brief encounters, like our short walk to the restaurant, offered just enough time for an open conversation with the safety of boundaries. Garnet and I fell in step together, having been seated at opposite ends of a long boardroom throughout the day's events. The intensity of our conversation must have been apparent to the rest of the group, as we soon found ourselves sauntering along behind everyone else. We had both seemed to understand that this was an opportunity to check in, but Garnet also had something else on his mind. He was telling me about an idea of writing a book that had been brewing within him.

That Garnet was thinking about writing a book wasn't surprising to me; I knew he'd been thinking of a way to share his beliefs and hard-earned lessons with the world for some time, and that by doing so, he might help others overcome their own challenges. But, as he explained, his vision for the book had evolved. Now, instead of writing the book for the entire world, he wanted to write it for my son, Keenan.

Over the course of our relationship, Garnet had formed a bond with Keenan, affectionately naming him "Keenan the Magnificent" during a shared dinner we'd all had one evening. The name stuck, not only because of how sincerely it was given, but because, at the age of six, Keenan adopted it as a title and began referring to himself in the third person. For Keenan, Garnet was part grandparent, part mentor, and part friend—and for Garnet, I think Keenan represented a version of himself in his formative years. Because of that, nurturing Keenan and helping him grow into his full potential had given Garnet a new sense of purpose; it seemed to be a way for him to transform the hardships he'd been through into meaningful lessons he could pass on directly (an expression of Garnet's deep commitment to generosity, which is a running theme throughout this book).

Garnet explained that by writing this book, he wanted to share Dan Sullivan's **Four Referability Habits** with Keenan. According to Dan Sullivan, co-founder of Strategic Coach®, the Four Referability Habits are:

1. Show up on time.
2. Do what you say.
3. Finish what you start.
4. Say please and thank you.

These were habits Garnet had learned the hard way, and to which he attributed much of his significant success. He had shared them with me as well, and we had both agreed they were powerful in their simplicity. Garnet and I had previously discussed how hard it could be to adhere to these tenets of conduct, no matter how basic they seemed—though we'd also agreed doing so consistently and without wavering could lead to magnificent results.

Still, Sullivan's four principles were not the end of the conversation; instead, they became more of a jumping-off point for Garnet and me to dive into deeper and more introspective waters than either of us (than I, at least) expected. As Garnet explained, he wanted *my* support to help bring this book to life. He needed someone with a background in social and psychological sciences to lend credibility to the impact of these lessons, yes—but more importantly, he needed someone to help him reflect on the moments and experiences we'd shared over the years, as we had such a unique relationship. When we first met, I was Garnet's coach and fitness trainer and our relationship had been strictly professional. Over time, however, it had evolved into a profound friendship—and finally, we were now officially choosing to become family to one another. (It was part of why we were in Vancouver in the first place.)

In Garnet's new vision, the arc of our relationship, and the many life-changing conversations we had, would become the book's new backbone. Our story would also be told primarily from my perspective—partly because Garnet had no interest in writing a traditional self-help book or aggrandizing his own success and partly because I could speak extensively to the impact our relationship had on me and my son, Keenan. By telling our story that way, I was in a unique position to provide other readers a lens through which they might glean their own insights.

While that day marked the beginning of our journey as co-authors, what followed were many other converging ideas and personal discoveries we couldn't have anticipated. After many drafts and iterations, we settled on the title, *17 Runs*, both as a nod to how our friendship had grown through training together, and because it was the age that Keenan would be when we gifted him the finished product.

As humans, we are natural storytellers, and through this journey, we found that much of what we thought we knew about ourselves and each other—which we thought might become a simple compilation of lessons learned—gradually turned into something much greater. But how could either of us have foreseen how personally transformational writing this book together would be?

In its final version, *17 Runs* tries to honor all the emotional and philosophical topics that Garnet and I discussed again and again for years (and still debate to this day). Rather than serving as any official guidebook to life's struggles, our hope is that this book will provoke real thought and discussion, becoming a source of comfort and inspiration to others by helping them outgrow limiting beliefs, find strength in their own chosen families, and learn to dream again. On another level, it is a very personal testament to the love and respect Garnet and I have for each other—first as friends, and finally, as chosen family.

—Olivia Chadwick, 2025

Prologue

I t would have been a great shame if Garnet and I hadn't met, as our heartfelt conversations taught us both so much about how to live with integrity. Looking back, however, missing out on all that growth is something that very much could've never happened.

When Garnet became my client, I was building up my personal training business, working mostly with CEOs like him. Garnet was training with a friend of mine, but Garnet's schedule was so unpredictable that he wound up canceling nearly half of their sessions on a regular basis. I don't know why, but that type of thing didn't bother me; I never minded much if my schedule fluctuated.

My friend knew I was pretty laid back when it came to that kind of thing, so she called me. "He's really nice," she said, "but I can't handle the inconsistency."

And so, the next Saturday, I had my first session with Garnet. I knew very little about him going into it, except that he'd made all his money from the insurance business—and, of course, that he could be unpredictable.

What I would find out over the course of the following year

is still hard for me to believe. We were born two-and-a-half decades apart on opposite sides of the globe. He was just over 50 when we met, and I was approaching 30; he's originally from Canada, and I'm from England. But our childhoods, and their sometimes-extreme difficulties, were uncannily similar and put us on the path to our unlikely meeting.

I found out about Garnet's childhood in bits and pieces, little by little. As I learned, he didn't like to talk about it for a variety of reasons: he didn't want to be pitied, and he didn't want anyone to feel they needed to treat him differently or give him anything he didn't think he'd earned. Above all, he didn't want to use his childhood as an excuse to not accomplish what he knew he was capable of. But what he did gradually tell me about his childhood was heartbreaking.

Garnet was born into poverty, the second oldest of six children. His mother was very young when she had him, and due in part to her age and circumstances, she could be cruel. She punished Garnet for things that were out of his control, such as his poor health, and sent his oldest sister to live elsewhere when she was only four years old. As an adolescent, just when he was beginning to break away from his family and find himself, he was sexually abused by a family friend, throwing him into a spiral of shame and self-loathing. From then on, he had become determined not to rely on anyone but himself.

He was intent on making his way into another kind of life, and he did. Garnet found financial success at a young age, before he turned 25. After taking out a loan, he bought a hotel and rapidly built wealth thanks to his natural knack for business and numbers. He got married and had two daughters, and for nearly two decades, things were on the upswing—but it didn't last. One right after the other, two of his siblings died by suicide, and his parents were so consumed by grief that he was left to pick up the pieces on his own.

Often the discussions Garnet and I had were a question of who would make the other cry first, as they were that intense and profound. As it turned out, both of our lives had been colored by similarly dark formative events, which is already rare; the likelihood of that *and* feeling a cosmic connection to one another on top of it, however, seemed practically unheard of.

The more I learned about Garnet, the more shocked I was, because my background contains many of the same hardships. My family was working-class, and when my parents got divorced, my father abandoned us and his responsibilities. I learned quickly to not make waves or trouble. I retreated into myself, which worked until it didn't. I developed an eating disorder and soon unearthed a memory of being molested by my uncle. For years, I ran from that truth, until I couldn't run anymore and eventually had to face up to the emotional devastation and trauma it caused. By that time, I'd suffered another blow; my sister, brilliant and tormented, took her own life at the age of 22.

As Garnet and I trained together and discovered these uncanny similarities, we opened up to one another more and more. We began talking about how we'd both been held back and motivated by the circumstances into which we were born; how they served us and hurt us at the same time. Since he was 20 years my senior, Garnet was further along in the healing process. He was also further along in business by many millions of dollars, despite having made some devastating mistakes along the way that almost cost him everything. Not wanting to see me go down the same path—and gradually becoming more of a friend than a client—he began somewhat inadvertently teaching me the life lessons he'd gained over the years (and this was long before we thought of co-authoring a book). Much of our training was running-based, and as often happens during that kind of physical activity, our walls came down throughout our training sessions.

Something Garnet and I discussed often was the idea of a family belief system. This isn't in reference to a set of religious beliefs, but rather the system of values in which we're raised.

He and I were both brought up to believe that we weren't lovable, that there was something wrong with us because we didn't fit into our families of origin. Some families encourage growth and change, but others live in fear of change and expect everyone to fall in line and do the same. For folks who grow up in those family systems, change can be extremely difficult.

But Garnet's deepest held belief was and still is that we are all capable of overcoming hardship and living the lives we're meant to live, as long as we are willing to put in the hard work of living with integrity. This had always been my belief as well, though I'd never put it in words so clearly before the two of us had met.

The more we discussed this idea, the more we realized many of the obstacles placed in our way as children had been or could be transformed or removed through intentional—and often difficult—steps. Those steps included things like learning how to dream again, developing good habits, identifying our *real* personal values, creating specific goals, and getting comfortable with discomfort. After discussing these topics countless times, we realized how much our conversations had been fundamentally changing who we were as people. Eventually, we wanted to share our discussions with others who were struggling and who might benefit from them in similar ways. The ultimate goal was to offer them the same tools and ideas we used and discussed to overcome our own limits and start living the lives we'd truly dreamed. As we saw it, if we could do it, so could anyone else.

As Garnet and I discovered in our real lives, we had to tear down our own walls with one another before we could transform for the better through our relationship. While writing this book together, we learned that the same principle applied between authors and readers. As Garnet once put it, "When you're open, you find people—but people need to know you're looking." We learned we couldn't just list important lessons or position ourselves as having all the answers.

Since revealing our own hardest moments was what allowed us to overcome them, we do the same here. In these pages, we offer only lessons earned through our own lived experience and on the authority of hard-won vulnerability—and hopefully not from a pulpit or any kind of soapbox. This means that as you read, any "lessons" (really, things for further consideration) will come through learning how Garnet and I broke down our own walls to develop our relationship.

This book takes place over the course of the first year that Garnet and I worked together. Some chapters represent single runs that are tied to a specific memory or moment—though often, Garnet and I continued discussing the topics of those runs for weeks after. After each of these sections, readers will find summaries of the major points we discussed, questions to reflect on, and exercises to try to help find a sense of direction.

In between these chapters, you'll find standalone vignettes from our lives that help explain where Garnet and I both come from beyond our relationship with one another. These are included for transparency and context, because each marks an instant in which our trajectories were irrevocably changed (though they are also a tribute to Mitch Albom's *Tuesdays with Morrie*, a book that inspired the both of us). Many of these pieces contain profoundly painful experiences we went through as well as obstacles we faced and how we overcame them. While the running chapters are told in a shared voice, in these vignettes, we speak about our lives from our own perspectives.

Finally, in the back of the book, you'll find additional resources—many of which we used ourselves—that we hope will help you on your path.

For me, this journey has been bumpy but life-changing. Years ago, I became disillusioned with the fitness industry and its hyperfocus on unrealistic body standards, exercise as pain or punishment, and losing weight as the ultimate marker of health. My personal and professional journey has included discovering the world of self-compassion and the desire to bring that message to as many people as I can (and during our time together, Garnet also helped me conceive of how I might pivot my business in that direction as well).

It hasn't always been easy—in fact, it's been profoundly difficult at times—but it has all taught me how much I'm capable of and what I still have left to do. In this book, we show you, the reader, the steps we took to discover who we truly were, what we wanted from life and how we might attain it— even and especially when it meant finding the integrity to define our lives ourselves and not by the values we inherited from our families of origin.

All told, Garnet and I did 200 runs together in our first year. We hope you will come along with us on some of them. By sharing the insights that helped us the most, we hope others will learn from our stories and avoid mistakes that might otherwise lead to unnecessary suffering. As we hope our story shows, anyone from any background can live a life they truly dream of —though it may require some initial discomfort and a lifelong commitment to integrity.

—Olivia Chadwick

1. Identifying and Removing Our Bricks

"If you are lost, may you understand that we are all lost, and still we are guided—by Strange Angels and Sleeping Giants, by our better and kinder natures, by the vibrant voice within the beat. May you follow that voice, for This is the way—the hero's journey, the life worth living, the reason we are here."

—Elizabeth Lesser

Date: October 1, 2011
Time: 5 a.m.
Session: 10

I n Saskatoon, Saskatchewan, the sun doesn't rise until past 8 a.m. from early fall through winter. As usual, on Monday, I woke up before everyone else in the house to get ready for a training session with Garnet.

We'd been working together for about a month, and I was slowly learning about him. As with all my clients, I spent the first few sessions getting to know him as best I could and determining what type of training regimen would be most effective for his level of physical fitness, his goals, and his personality.

One of his primary aims was to increase his cardiovascular strength, so we'd been focusing so far on running. That morning, I'd planned a four-mile outdoor endurance run.

When I looked out the window into the pitch black, though, I realized with mild panic that the night before, we'd been buried in snow.

As I dug through my closet for an extra layer, I tried to come up with a back-up plan in case Garnet wasn't up for the blistering cold. Once I found another layer and threw it on, I crept from the bedroom to the kitchen, trying to be as quiet as possible. My partner, our three-year-old son, and the tenant who rented out our basement were all still asleep. The last thing I wanted to do was wake up my toddler, which would have significantly delayed me and irked my partner—and our tenant too, I imagined.

This was how most of my mornings went, and it usually meant I was getting ready in darkness. I looked at the clock: 4:45 a.m. Garnet's apartment was only seven minutes from our house, but I didn't want to risk being late. I grabbed a bottle of water, skipped breakfast and coffee, and left.

Garnet lived in a beautiful eight-story condo building that abutted the southern banks of the South Saskatchewan River. He'd lived there for a few months in the wake of a divorce from his first wife. They'd been married for over 30 years and had two children together; but as so often happens, they grew apart. Although he was sparse with details, I felt from my conversations with him that the adjustment had been difficult and that he experienced it as a personal failure.

Garnet was waiting for me in the lobby when I arrived. He was dressed in crisp running clothes and, as I'd noticed he always did, he appeared as pristine as if he'd just showered even though we were about to work out. In each of our sessions, he never had even a millimeter of stubble on his head, which he kept clean-shaven. This stood out to me because in my experience, there's an association between success and putting effort into personal appearance—particularly at a time of day when it would be easy to let it slide. It demonstrated self-respect and a commitment to setting the bar high at all times, regardless of the activity or situation.

Garnet waved when I walked in, and his sky blue, bright eyes were friendly.

"Garnet, I was planning on an outdoor run today," I said as I approached. "Are you up for it? It's pretty cold out there."

"Oh sure," he said. "I don't mind the cold. We'll warm up as we go."

I'd already noticed that Garnet was game for going outside in this type of weather, but it still surprised me. The thermometer registered negative four degrees Fahrenheit, a temperature so frigid that some people who don't live with winters like this would consider it incredibly uncomfortable at best, and potentially harmful at worst. It requires deep dedication to one's health goals, but more than that, it requires the willingness and ability to overcome negative internal thoughts which insist—quite convincingly!—that it would be much more pleasant to stay inside.

We started on some pre-run stretches in the lobby.

"How's your morning so far?" he asked, leaning against the wall as I instructed him to do, extending each foot one at a time.

"Good," I said almost automatically, trying not to think about everyone who was still sound asleep at my house.

"Glad to hear it," he said, nodding with a firm smile.

We set out down a running trail we both liked, which meandered along the edge of the water. It was quiet and serene, and at this time of the morning, it felt like we were the only people in the world. My goal for that day's session was to get him to run about a quarter-mile further than he'd gone so far, and when we were done, we'd head to the gym in his building for weight training and more stretching.

As we made our way towards the trail, we chatted about what was going on in our lives. This was a routine we'd quickly fallen into; like me, Garnet preferred to skip small talk and get to know people on a deeper level sooner rather than later. He'd been very open with me about his health journey so far. He'd lost over 100 pounds over the past several years, mainly through changing his eating habits. He shared a bit about some of the challenges he was having with his soon-to-be ex-wife, and even some anecdotes about his childhood, which, from what I could gather, had been very difficult.

Likewise, he knew about my goals with my personal training business and my estrangement from several members of my family. I was also fairly open about some health problems my son was having, which my partner and I were still in the process of understanding.

Since Garnet tended to run on the slower side, I paced myself to meet him where his body naturally wanted to be. We passed sleepy buildings along the edge of the frozen water, our breath visible in the frigid air. As we jogged, I told Garnet about the day I had ahead, which resembled most of my days as of late.

"After this, I'll try to get home in time to help get Keenan to daycare, then I've got back-to-back training sessions till 5:30," I said. "I'll go home for dinner, then off to the Pilates studio to teach for a couple more hours."

I related that I did all of this to keep a roof over our head and food on the table, but it was also very important to me to always be working towards a bigger goal: taking my business to the next level, working on myself, deepening or improving my relationship. My partner and I had a bumpy start; after dating on and off for years, we wound up pregnant shortly after I graduated from college. It changed both of our life plans completely. Still, I never gave up on my dream to advance in my career and make a better life for my son than the life I had had. In this way, my partner and I were different; he's a hard worker and a deeply kind person, but like a lot of people in their twenties, he hadn't found his passion and struggled with the demands of adult life.

That meant I was the primary breadwinner and he spent more time caring for our child. But after I worked for a few years, we had enough money for a down payment on a house. It wasn't the biggest or newest, but it was ours: a charming, 1,000-square foot bungalow in a quiet, residential neighborhood. I thought eventually we would move on to something more. I had dreams of scaling my business and reaching more people with a message of empowerment, and in my heart, I believed I could do it. I just wasn't sure where to start.

And this all came tumbling out while Garnet and I ran. It was unusual; typically I was the person listening during training sessions. My clients often treated me like a trainer and therapist rolled into one, which I didn't mind at all. I enjoyed getting to know them as human beings. But I was rarely on the talking end. It was different with Garnet in part because he asked questions and then actually listened to the answers, and because we shared so many core values.

Either way, as I blathered on, I insisted I was doing everything I could to make our lives work and to set a good example for my child. On some level, though, I suspected I was being held back by fear.

"You know, Olivia," Garnet said between puffs of white breath, "most people don't realize they can overcome their family's belief system. Meaning, you can make changes in your life to live the way you want, rather than just following the path you were raised to."

We rounded a snowy corner, and the black sky before us began to turn a deep blue.

"That's what you did, and it's what I did," Garnet continued. "We both came from difficult childhoods and made choices along the way to set us in new directions. It's called 'brick removal': the determination to overcome the obstacles that are in your path, put there by your parents, their parents, the system in which you were raised, friends, social media, and so forth, one by one. Once you recognize the obstacles, it's a question of being prepared for the discomfort you'll feel as you move beyond your past patterns."

I'd never heard my life framed that way before, and it brought me up so short that I almost stopped in my tracks. I grew up in a working-class family in England and was the first person to go to college. My trajectory didn't strike me as unusual; it had felt very natural, even though it deviated from the example my family set for me. What happened then was that once my personal training business plateaued, I didn't know what to do next—and didn't trust myself to figure it out.

I'd inherited this brick, the feeling that I didn't deserve to be successful. It was a belief that limited my idea of myself and my capabilities, and it was holding me back from growing and reaching my full potential. It was self-sabotage, and it meant that I didn't even know how to take the first steps that would allow me to learn how to pursue my dreams or have my needs met. In fact, this message of not being worthy of more than what I was raised with was so strong in my mind and produced such powerful and loud negative thoughts that it was hard to even hear my own voice and desires.

After we'd run about two miles, Garnet and I paused to

drink some water and catch our breath. It was almost time for us to turn around, so I gradually started to break into a run again before we lost momentum.

I turned his ideas over in my mind. "It's almost like you have to become a different person, isn't it?" I said. "Challenging those old belief systems means we can create a new reality."

"Yes," he replied. "We'll always play those records in our heads, the ones that were put there when we were kids, but you have to create your own perspective, which will likely be in conflict, to a large degree, with your family values and how they were brought up and lived their life."

I thought about how scared I'd been to move away from home, even though I'd known it was the right thing to do. That was when I began defining my values for myself. It was the removal of my first brick. Now, it was as if I was still carrying around the others and putting them in my own way because that's how I felt comfortable.

"Most people don't understand what it means to move beyond what they've seen and imagine something different," Garnet continued. "Your innate ability to do so means you're on the right track." As he said it, the sun was starting to peek over the horizon, hitting the exterior of Garnet's building in a way that turned its blue glass walls into an iridescent rose-pink.

———

When I got back to my house that day, Keenan was already awake. He was joyful and delighted to see me, and I gave him a big hug. My partner was awake too, and the two of them were playing with stuffed animals on the rug in the living room. With Garnet's words still echoing in my head, I could feel myself beginning to soften.

I thought about what a brick really is. It's hard, yes, and it's heavy, and it has the potential to weigh someone down. But it's not impenetrable. If I wanted to remove a brick, I simply needed to understand what it was made of, believe in my power to remove it, develop the skills to do so, and be willing to keep trying—maybe multiple times if I didn't get rid of it on my first attempt. I needed to create an internal voice that questioned why I kept it around in the first place.

These were all steps I knew I could take. Old beliefs can create a reality, but they don't create the *only* reality.

When my morning session started with Garnet that day, I felt unsure about my efforts and the direction in which I was heading. But now that I had this new language for what I was dealing with, I could feel something beginning to shift. *Maybe I'm already doing a lot of the right things, and I just need to be a little bit gentler with myself,* I thought. I didn't know where all this was going, but I did know I'd already begun the work and that at the end of the day, it was up to me.

Things to Think On
Learning to Identify and Remove Your Own Bricks

> *Note: While the runs present pivotal moments in our relationship, the truth is that they do so in a condensed way. In reality, these discussions lasted for weeks or months, and some are still ongoing. As such, each of these sections are summaries of real, ongoing discussions we had rather than prescriptions to follow or overly tidy conclusions. These are the real things we thought about and struggled with while writing; if these sections don't resonate, it may be best to reread rather than prematurely treating them as instructions.*

What we will call "bricks" are limiting beliefs, values, ideas about yourself, and notions about how to behave that are instilled in us by our parents, family members, caregivers, partners and other adults or community members that we let influence us. These messages often get passed down through generations—beliefs about what we can and cannot do, be, or ask for that were learned by our great-grandparents, grandparents, and parents—and then ourselves.

Some examples of bricks could be:

- We have a desire to perform in front of an audience, but have received the message that our need to be seen is immodest or vain, or that we aren't good enough to "make it."
- We have emotional needs that are not being met, such as the need to be comforted by loved ones, the need to be heard, or the need to feel understood. We've received that message that those needs are "not real" or are selfish and ungrateful.
- We've expressed a desire to pursue a career that would require a lot of schooling, but we've heard that our education would take a long time or cost too much.
- If we take a break or some much-needed rest, we're lazy.
- Our partner suggests that we aren't good to them because their mother/father/grandmother did things differently.
- We have dreams of succeeding in business but struggled academically in school; as such, we've somehow internalized that we aren't "smart enough."

We all have "bricks" of one type or another, but if we look at our life and see that we're not the person we want to be, we can stop and think: What obstacles were in our path, and have we sought the advice we need on how to overcome them?

If we feel there's something missing in our lives, that life does not feel real to us, or that there is a lot more on offer some-where, we shouldn't blame others—instead, we should notice where we have bricks. What are the ideas or beliefs we were raised with that are now preventing us from knowing ourselves and what we want? What is preventing us from taking action?

The ability to see our bricks without judgment, understand why they're there, and become open to learning how to remove them is called self-awareness raising, and it is the most powerful and impactful step in becoming who we want to be and building the life we want.

Here are some tools we used to notice our bricks and begin removing them that you can use as well:

- **Read**. There are many great resources available to help identify beliefs that no longer serve us, such as the books listed in the Appendix.
- **Talk to people you admire** about their beliefs, keeping in mind that you could adopt those beliefs as well.
- **Taking cues from real people you've met** —not social media, because that is not reality.
- **Journal**. By doing this, we can write down a vision for our lives—as lofty and fantastic as we want!—and begin to hone in on how we might create that vision. We should be specific; for example, we should say, "I want to have a 90 average," not "I want to do better at school."
- **Notice**. What are the people around us doing that we might like to do? How can we learn from those actions and mindsets and make them our own?
- **Remember: you are who you hang out with**. If our friends are content to stay stagnant in life, they might be reinforcing our bricks—or creating new ones.
- **Visualize the real you, who you could be**. Creating a mental image in our head helps us get where we need to go.

- **Remember that brick removal is a lifelong process**. Our goal is progress, not perfection.

None of these things are simple or easy. They will likely be very challenging and part of a lifelong process since once one brick is gone, we find another, and another. But the first step to brick removal is recognizing that limiting beliefs exist and *can be changed*. Simply acknowledging this concept is an important first step.

If you'd told me 30 years ago that I would have a career as a personal trainer, I would have looked at you sideways.

Like Garnet, my mother was young when she had my sister and me. My older sister, Cassie, was born when my mother was twenty-one, and I followed just a year later. We lived in a small town south of London, in a house across the street from my mother's sister and her family. For generations, we'd been a working-class, blue collar family. It was understood that at 16, after graduating from the UK's equivalent of high school, you would start working. That expectation was solidly in place for my sister and me.

However, for the first few years of my life, my family did well and it looked like we might move up from our low-income roots. My father sold high-end cars and made a lot of money in a short amount of time. It was a huge shift for both my parents, who each grew up in blue collar families. They rode the high for as long as they could; my father used to wear flashy suits and take my sister and me to school in a Lamborghini just for fun.

But by the time I was eight, my father overfilled his proverbial bucket and it caused a catastrophic disaster in our lives. He and his business partner ordered an unfathomable number of cars to sell at the same moment that a massive recession hit England. No one was interested in luxury goods, and almost as quickly as the money came, it disappeared.

The strain on my parent's relationship was too much. They were loving towards my sister and me but horribly abusive to each other, physically and emotionally. They finally split up when I was nine, but the problems didn't stop there.

My mother was always very resourceful and a hard worker —something I think I inherited from her—and she began taking jobs cleaning houses. In doing so, she taught me that hard work is a form of agency, and that no job was beneath you if it allowed you to live. As a single mom with a high school education raising two girls, it would have been easy—and normal—for her to claim welfare, but she didn't. She wanted a life that provided more than what welfare allowed, and she was prepared to work hard for that. She never had shame about what she did to make money. In fact, she ensured that she held high standards in her work and was reliable. Because of this work ethic, she got well-paying jobs from clients that often became good friends. Her ability to model resourcefulness, responsibility, work ethic were integral to her self-respect.

As my mother was working as hard as she could, my father was struggling. He could not afford to pay the child support he owed, and in an effort to make him do so, my mother withheld him from visiting us.

My mother wasn't the only person my father couldn't pay. He owed money to suppliers and others whom he couldn't pay back. Faced with bankruptcy and the shame of not being able to see his children, my father, who had dual citizenship in Canada, left for British Columbia.

It would be years before I saw him again.

After my parents' divorce, I quickly identified and carved out a role for myself in the family. My sister had an extremely difficult childhood—I suspect she had bipolar disorder, but in the 1990s, no one knew enough to diagnose her properly—and with my mother so preoccupied with trying to keep her safe and also putting food on the table, I became the strong one, the child who didn't make waves, who took care of herself and stayed out of the way.

After my father left England for Canada, I embodied that role even more. I worked, never complained, and got excellent grades.

What no one could see was how I was falling apart inside. By the time I was 14, I'd discovered the best way of all to avoid causing trouble was to disappear. And like so many girls my age, I knew how to make that happen.

I don't recall ever telling anyone that I was on a diet. But I do remember learning the recipe for weight loss from Just 17 magazine. My family couldn't afford to buy it often, so I devoured it in a convenience store aisle before school, and it was there that I received my first education on the "perfect" 1,200-calorie diet. Of course, eating disorders are about much more than weight; the medical and psychiatric fields still don't have a solid understanding of the etiological causes. Often—including in my case—there is a history of abuse, trauma, personality, and other factors that cause dysfunction in the brain. The mental illness that we call anorexia nervosa—my diagnosis—is a complex way of coping that is projected onto the body.

Over the course of the next two years, my behaviors became more and more severe. At the height of my disease, I would get up early, before anyone else, and run for 45 minutes. I would have two Weetabix with water or no-fat milk and a cup of tea for breakfast—obsessive adherence to routine is part of the disease—and would attempt to eat no more than 800 calories throughout the day.

The number on the scale dropped lower and lower.

Like my sister, I had no way of being diagnosed. Most experts believed at that time that eating disorders were caused by a fad diet gone wrong or, at worst, a desire for control. These oversimplified and incorrect assumptions only caused more girls like me to suffer and, in some cases, to die.

My family only knew how to shame me into obedience, and their attempts to do so in an effort to get me to eat sailed right over my head. My sense was that they didn't want to try to understand what was going on with me but just wanted it to end. Their method was to stay silent about it, which—although they didn't mean it this way—felt to me like being shunned and ignored in my time of need. But nothing compared to the feeling of getting smaller and smaller, of consuming less and less— taking up as little space as possible, existing solely in my own little world.

Still, my mother did take me to a counselor once, and it was there that I uncovered a memory I'd long since buried: that of my uncle sexually abusing me. The memory was crystal clear, and I told my mother about it. In response, she reminded me how strong I was and how strong she was. Her sister and brother-in-law were not as strong, she said. They wouldn't be able to handle it. We would. And because of that, we needed to keep it to ourselves.

Her implied request—that I stay silent about this, at least as far as telling the rest of my family—ate away at me. It became intolerable, holding such a massive secret and trying to appear "okay" on the outside. I needed to break free of this impossible demand. All I needed was a tiny spark of vivacity, one moment in which I expressed a desire to save my own life.

I discovered it one afternoon at my uncle's house.

At the time, international phone calls were expensive, and we only made them at my aunt's house. Somehow, I wound up on the phone with my father; I can't remember if he called me or I called him. We hadn't spoken in months, but suddenly, inspiration rose up inside me.

The previous year, I'd asked if I could come live with him in Canada. He'd responded by saying that he would consider it if and when I graduated from school. I'd done so, and I realized this was my moment. I could not stay in England, could not finish high school and start work, as was expected, and I could not live across the street from those family members anymore.

Speaking to my dad through a fuzzy connection, I reiterated my request to come live with him. As he deliberated with his new wife, I waited, chewing my fingernails and listening to their muffled voices. Soon he came back to the receiver. They agreed it would be fine—I could leave England and move to Canada with them.

My cousin was standing close enough to hear it all and began to push back. Later, I'd find out how devastated and resentful she was that I got to leave.

"You can't go!" she said. "We're your family!"

Soon my mother chimed in as well, and it felt like a chorus of voices yelling at me. It was my breaking point. I held the receiver away from my head and screamed, "I have to go! I have to live my life! Let me go!" They were the truest words I'd ever spoken.

It was profoundly out of character for me, the child who knew in her bones that it was her role to play the good girl. I may never understand what I tapped into in that moment, but I'm forever grateful, because in the end, it saved my life.

Within a few months, I was on an airplane.

2. Good Habits Are the Foundation of Success

Dan Sullivan's Four Referability Habits:

Show up on time.
Do what you say.
Finish what you start.
Say please and thank you.

Date: November 12, 2011
Time: 5 a.m.
Session: 25

After our first month working together, Garnet and I began to hit a stride. I could already see his endurance and strength increasing, and I knew he trusted my coaching philosophy. Mid-way through November, I wanted to push him a bit further than usual on our run.

Part of this was standard training procedure: incrementally increasing distance and speed.

But Garnet had recently tossed out the idea of running the Kananaskis 100 Mile Relay that following year, a stunning but difficult race that takes participants over the highest paved highway in Canada. Participants form small teams, and each person tackles ten miles. The legs vary greatly in terms of difficulty; some include rapidly escalating elevation, and some are hillier than others.

We both wanted to get a sense of which leg of the relay Garnet could do if we chose to sign up, so my plan for the session was to challenge him with the environment. There was a stair set on our trail where we could do some quick footwork, as well as hills to work on turnover and strength.

The weather was perfect for our run. The temperature was in the high 60s, and the sun had been up for nearly an hour by the time I arrived. As we warmed up in the lobby, I checked in with Garnet to see how he was feeling. Since he traveled so much and often slept for five hours or fewer, I liked to give him the chance to tell me if I should hold back on pushing him.

"How's your energy this morning?" I asked.

"I'm feeling just fine, Olivia," he said. "How are *you*?"

"I'm fine as well, Garnet," I said with a laugh. "Let's get going."

Since an important element of building good running technique is doing a deliberate and prolonged warm-up, we started with a slow jog. It was a practice that helped with long-term gains, though it can feel repetitive and even tedious. It can also make people feel tired before the workout has even begun and frustrated over doing something that doesn't give them the satisfaction of running farther or faster than usual.

For those reasons, I wasn't all that surprised when Garnet began to show his exasperation.

"Aren't we training for a race, here?" he said.

"You know you could get hurt if you don't warm up correctly," I said. "You need to build the habit of slowing down and doing this correctly if you want your health to improve over time."

He huffed a bit, then became quiet. We continued down to the river and along a grassy path. After five more minutes, I stopped him next to a clearing.

"All right," I said. "Side lunges, then front lunges. Let's go."

"Is this to increase my flexibility? Because you know I'm a stickman. It's never going to work," he said.

"No. This prepares your joints and neuromuscular system for running, so you don't snap into pieces like a real stickman might."

In fitness training, these kinds of exercises are called dynamic drills, and like slow warm-ups, they were never client favorites. Still, I was curious about Garnet's resistance. I knew how hard he'd worked on his health journey, losing nearly 100 pounds and completely changing his eating habits. In business, he'd applied a similar mindset, building a multi-million dollar organization from the ground up. In order to accomplish those things, he had to have quit some bad habits and developed new ones. Our work together was just another way of building good habits. I wondered if I could coax him into connecting the dots.

"Garnet," I said, "what are the habits that helped you pivot and grow your business? How do you keep yourself on track when there are things you don't *want* to do but *need* to do?"

"Well, I think you're implying that a person can't be successful without good habits, and you're right about that," he said.

I waited for him to say more, but he fell silent. I prodded. "What has that journey looked like so far for you?"

"For me, the first thing I had to do was break my bad habits," he said. "The first one was smoking. I was smoking two packs of cigarettes a day and developing all types of precursors for terrible diseases, and I decided I didn't want that anymore."

He paused to take a few deep breaths and drink some water. "Did I ever tell you about the moment I finally decided to get help?" he asked.

"No," I said.

"It wasn't that big of a deal. It wasn't Moses on the hill with a burning bush. It happened at the Toronto Airport. I had to run from one end of the airport to the other, dragging my suitcase along behind me, and by the time I got to my gate, I was covered in sweat and completely breathless. It was humiliating. I was disgusted with myself. I weighed more than 300 pounds, and I'd finally had enough. I was really getting afraid of what would happen if I didn't do something."

I was surprised by that image. The Garnet I knew was clean-shaven and punctual, with good eating habits and a commitment to his health. It was hard to imagine him any other way. I was even more curious than I was at the outset. I'd expected him to say that he started eating more vegetables or incorporating more exercise, but what he was describing sounded like an entire overhaul of his lifestyle. That type of change is rare. No one really knows what's at play psychologically when humans successfully change the way they live, and most of us struggle with it mightily. I'd seen many highly successful, highly motivated clients fail over and over to alter deeply ingrained behavioral patterns, no matter how much they truly wanted to change. I wondered if Garnet could articulate his process.

"How did you do it?" I asked him as I started doing high knees, gesturing to him that he should follow along.

"First, I had to get brutally honest with myself. I had to stop all the self-deception, dissociation, denial, and avoidance of the things in my life that were holding me back. It was one of the most painful exercises I'd ever done."

"I can imagine," I said. "I think that first step is the hardest part."

"Next, I went to a doctor. She told me, 'Garnet, I can tell you what to do, but don't expect me to be your mother.' That one sentence was transformative. It was the thing I needed to hear at the moment I needed to hear it. I recognized that no one was going to do this for me."

"You had to take responsibility."

"Yes. It was humiliating to hear, but it drove me to the next step, which was to see a sports psychologist. That's where I really began examining my self-defeating behavior. I also joined Strategic Coach, which is a leadership training program, and they kept bringing up *habits*. It seemed like everyone around me was talking about habits.

"What they said at Strategic Coach, and what really stuck with me, was that you can't quit a bad habit, you can only replace it with a better one. So for example, when I quit smoking, I had to change my morning routine completely. I used to get up in the morning, have a cigarette. Drink a coffee, have another cigarette. Then I'd have breakfast, another cigarette. Shower, another cigarette. And so on and so forth. I had to do something different in each of those moments."

"What did you do?" I said.

"I didn't have coffee. I went right into the shower."

"You quit coffee and cigarettes at the same time?"

"No, I quit having coffee *at that time*. I changed my routine so that I showered, and then I had breakfast. When I went to work, I went a different way, because if I went the same way, I would relate each familiar sight to the cigarettes I smoked in the car. It took a while for the habit of smoking at particular times to go away. One of the tricks I learned is to take very small steps every day. I tracked them and started to see how they were building up over time. Before I knew it, I'd made these major life changes."

"That's a behavioral therapy approach," I said. "Change the behavior, change the reality."

"Well, you know the psychological reasons for it. All I know is that within a year, I was a different person, with all different habits."

We began to run, with leaves falling all around us. As always, the crunching sounds took me back to my childhood, when I loved to step on leaves as I walked to school.

"What about you, Olivia?" Garnet said. "How did you make big changes in your life?"

His question snapped me out of my reverie. I often asked clients questions about their lives, but it was uncommon for them to turn the inquiry back at me.

As soon as I thought about it, though, I realized I didn't have a good answer. Garnet was able to outline the ways he'd turned his life around, but I couldn't. When I enrolled in college, I barely understood the Canadian education system; I just knew that I needed to keep going to school to get where I wanted in life. I landed in personal training because it came naturally to me, and I was able to build up clientele. Then, I worked as hard as I could to grow my business. But when Garnet asked *how* I'd made those big changes, what was at play underneath it all, I realized that what I'd done was hit the gas pedal on my life as a teenager and I'd never taken my foot off it again.

In fact, I was still pressing down on the accelerator. Garnet picked up on my hesitation.

"How about this," he said. "What are some of the good habits you've implemented in your life?"

I breathed a sigh of relief at not having to figure out an

answer to his first question, although I made a mental note to think about it later.

"I think most of my good habits center around feeling my best," I said. "I want to show up for people with enthusiasm and optimism, so I do things to support that outcome. That includes a lot of behaviors. I protect my sleep by having a regular bedtime. I read every day. I practice relaxation techniques."

"Those are all important."

"They are. And you know what's funny? Most people think I love exercise and that it's easy for me, but that's not what drives me to be physically active. I like how exercise makes me *feel*, so I've developed the habit of getting up at 5 a.m. to do it."

"That's wonderful," said Garnet. "And you know what? That's the same reason I'm always ready to go when you get here. It's just a habit that I've formed. There are other things I wish I'd known when I was making some of those big changes in my life, like how to surround myself with kind, supportive people or that discomfort is part of change. I white-knuckled through it, but I'd do some things differently in hindsight."

————

We finished our run and went to the gym in Garnet's building to cool down with some stretching. As I nudged him along, I also tried to get him to tell me more about his habit-building techniques.

"You mentioned earlier that you replaced old habits with new ones," I said. "I'm so curious about that. How do you do it?"

"It's simple," he said. "You write down all your bad habits on a sheet of paper and come up with something to replace each of them. Then you decide which ones you're going to tackle first. You can't change everything all at once, so you decide which one you're going to work on first, and second, and third, and you track your progress. It's important that the steps are very small—we grossly overestimate our ability to change. And we have to celebrate the small things, because if you do something small and stick to it for even ten days, it'll create energy and momentum in a particular direction. Then the next small change will be easier."

Garnet's process reminded me of something I'd learned in graduate school that came up often with my clients: excuses, and all the ways our minds come up with them.

"When I'm trying to change a habit, I try to remember that my brain *wants* to hold on to my old habits," I said. "It's afraid of change, and so it comes up with excuses that sound deceptively plausible, like 'I have to make dinner soon, I don't have enough time for a walk,' or 'It would be rude of me to turn down that cake.' My rule for my clients is that nine times out of ten, you need to do the new thing regardless of what those excuses are telling you. Of course, that won't work if we're talking about addictions or other problems that require professional help. But when it comes to day-to-day changes, we need to be smarter than our own minds."

Things to Think On
The Steps to Building Good Habits

When we don't have good habits, it's hard for us to get anywhere in life. They are the basic requirements for changing our reality, but the good news is habits aren't qualities some people are born with and others aren't. They're a series of repeated actions and behaviors that anyone can build.

Habits come from doing things that are simple but might not be easy. For instance, getting up at 5 a.m. to exercise is hard but not complicated. Why is it hard? Because we're tired and our mind is making up excuses to stay in bed. Our only job is to thank our mind for its input and to tell it we're getting up anyway.

Fortunately, there are steps we can take to build good habits —and change bad ones.

Turning Bad Habits Into Good Habits

Remembering that every good habit is simply the transformation of a bad habit, we can follow a system to begin that transformation:

1. Identify the bad habits we want to change.

- Bad habits are habits we want to stop doing, such as spending too much time on social media, using drugs or alcohol at parties, or buying into the myth that being a rugged individual makes us strong, and trying to do everything ourselves. For anyone reading this and thinking, *Oh yeah, I can do this on my own,* you can't—no one can. Successful people rely on others to help them.

2. Identify which bad habits cause us the most pain. That's where we should begin.

3. Identify good habits that can replace the habits identified in Step 2. Some examples:

- Social media is keeping us up at night, causing us to underperform, be exhausted the next day, and feel depressed. Instead of keeping our phones next to the bed, we can put them in another room, or we can ask a family member to keep them out of sight for us.
- Relying too heavily on alcohol to get through stressful situations (or social situations). We can start telling people around us that we're taking a break from alcohol—and then actually do it.
- Feeling stuck in a rut in our favorite activity or class. Instead of spinning our wheels alone, we can ask for help, whether it's from a parent, a coach, or a teacher.

4. We can list out the small steps we need to take to get us to our new goal and when we're going to take each one.

5. We set ourselves up for success to take those steps by:

- Ensuring we have everything we need to make these incremental changes. Have we identified a place to leave our phones at night? Have we figured out who we'll ask for help?
- Planning for the unexpected. If we plan to not drink at Friday night's party, what will we say if someone pressures us?

6. We can track our progress as we go in a notebook, an app, a whiteboard—whatever is most convenient and gets us motivated. Our aim is progress, not perfection.

It's easy to get discouraged by how long it takes to change a habit, because so much of the work is incremental—one small step at a time. But as human beings, we are only capable of making small changes, one at a time, if we want them to stick. Learning and implementing good habits is a lifelong process, so none of us will get there overnight. Even so, that transformation is something that is more than within our power—no matter who we are.

I was born in Bracken, Saskatchewan, a farming town near the Montana border that had a population of fewer than 50 people. My family on my mother's side farmed sheep, and my mother was just 18 years old when she married my father and had me. Coming from an upbringing in which physical ability was necessary for survival, she was terrified and confused when I emerged sickly and uninterested in eating.

Early on, I showed signs of respiratory difficulties, which would develop into severe asthma. Inhalers didn't yet exist, so children in the throes of asthma attacks were put in oxygen tents to recover, and I was no exception. Over time, I grew isolated from other children. If I tried to run, I would lose my breath—and my life at home would get worse as my mother's frustration and desperation increased.

With no tools, physical or psychological, to cope with her ill child, my mother's fear quickly twisted into anger. She began calling me lazy, ignoring me when my asthma came on. Sometimes, she would simply put me in my room, letting me gasp for air alone.

Gradually, all four of my other siblings arrived, and with five children, my mother's capacity for dealing with me shrank to nothing. She verbally attacked all of us as children at the slightest provocation. Then came the physical violence, directed at whoever happened to be in her path.

Every Sunday, my family would eat dinner together, and it was an event I came to dread. As opposed to being a time for my parents and siblings to come together and discuss their weeks, bond and laugh, it turned into a time for my mother to express her anger and disappointment.

One night, she directed her anger towards my father, as she did from time to time. He spent too much time at church, he didn't earn enough money, he didn't discipline us enough. My father—a quiet man by nature—waited for her to take a breath.

"Elaine," he said, "we don't have to do this in front of the kids. We can do this later." She ignored him, eventually getting so enraged that she threw something in his direction.

As upsetting as it was, it was also a moment I would never forget. My father had shown my siblings and me that rage and violence did not have to be the answer. A person could remain calm and try to control the situation—whether it worked or not.

But at field day, things escalated to a point of no return.

I was with my family at a field day when my wheezing began. I was five years old, and I knew what was coming: an asthma attack. I also knew I didn't want to tell my parents. They were in the middle of a baseball game, and my mother had no tolerance for me showing what she called "weakness." Still, as my breaths became more and more shallow, I soon found myself gasping for air. I considered my choices: keep gasping, and who knew what would happen, or tell my parents and risk my mother's wrath. Out of a sense of survival, I finally chose the latter.

I went to my parents as my face was turning blue, and my mother carried me to the car and put me in the backseat—but instead of getting in, she closed me inside, alone. As the door clicked shut, she took my father's hand. I heard her say, "Let's go play another game."

Lying on the floor in the hot vehicle gasping for breath, I was certain I was going to die.

After the game, my parents finally took me to the hospital. Panicked, the doctors gave me a shot of adrenaline to get me breathing normally. Soon after, I was put in another room, where I vomited from the medication while my parents went home without me.

It would be the last time I went to my mother for help. In fact, at that moment, I decided I would never rely on anyone else again.

———

Over the next few years, I was in and out of the hospital often. My breathing difficulties necessitated routine care, and I would regularly have to stay there for a few days or a week. It could have been dreary and lonely, but I found kindness and hope in some of the hospital's caregivers—the nurses.

As the days went by, the nurses began to teach me things: how to make my bed neatly, to tuck the corners of my sheets in crisp folds. Some of them brought me books, including The Hardy Boys *and* The Adventures of Tom Sawyer. *My parents jumped in at times, too, bringing me other stories to read, and it was through all those fictional worlds that I first learned that a different kind of life might be possible.*

Though I'd decided to stop letting people in, I still recognized and found deep gratitude for the nurses' compassion. It would stay with me for the rest of my life.

By the time I was 13, I moved to a new town with my family. Though I still suffered from asthma, I had found new ways to cope with the solitude. I continued to read voraciously and started taking a raft out on the local pond, where I would spend hours imagining I was Tom Sawyer on the Mississippi River.

At home, things were as bad as they'd always been, but now, I had the option to leave. There was still no money, though; my parents worked, but didn't make much. My father was a railway agent and then worked for the credit union, and my mother became a hairdresser when I was 10.

Soon, I began to spend time at a local shop run by a friend of my father's. At first, it was a welcome respite from the bullying I endured from the other kids, and I was glad to while away the afternoon hours there instead of at home or in town. But after some time, my father's friend began acting in ways that seemed too personal. With no one to turn to, I accepted it as perhaps normal; after all, this was a well-respected businessman and family friend.

The abuse that followed happened within months, though I told no one. I internalized the man's actions, feeling profound shame and embarrassment. I began to question everything— about myself and who, if anyone, I could trust. I had only just begun to see a way out before something was dragging me down again.

After moving out of my parents' home at the age of 17, I immediately found work at the Canadian Imperial Bank of Commerce. By then, my asthma had disappeared, and I had a clear picture of how I wanted my life to be: different from how I grew up. I found I had a knack for numbers, and I moved fast through the ranks. Still, something inside me knew that I wanted to have my own business. It gnawed at me, no matter how high I rose or what position I was promised as the years went on.

In Bracken, Saskatchewan, the person with the most money in town was a man who owned a hotel. Without giving it much more thought than that, I decided that was what I would do. When I was 20, a friend of mine and I devised a scheme to borrow $30,000. With that money, we purchased our first hotel, and within a few months, I'd bought my friend out.

After two years, I sold the first hotel and got into real estate, buying another hotel and then another. Finally, I thought, things were starting to look up.

3. Dreams Let Our Imagination Run Wild

"The breeze at dawn has secrets to tell you. Don't go back to sleep. You must ask for what you really want."

—*Rumi*

Date: December 2, 2011
Time: 6 a.m.
Session: 37

The park was filling up when I arrived. Kids were on the playground, early risers were getting ready for a workout, and couples were admiring the icicles hanging from trees.

It was Saturday morning, and I was there to join Garnet on his weekly run. But this time, it wasn't just us. Every weekend, Garnet met up with a group of friends to exercise. They jogged together down the river's edge, catching up with one another as they went. Most had children who still lived at home, so it was a time in their lives when socializing had to be squeezed in alongside another productive activity. Some of these friends had been running with Garnet for years and had become his close inner circle. I knew that his inviting me to these runs was an indication, in his way, that he was starting to consider me a friend. That meant so much to me that I wouldn't have dreamed of not showing up.

That weekend, the whole troop was there: Heather, the nurse; Moira, the businesswoman; and Lori, the artist, who was always playing peacemaker when people had disagreements. As I approached, I also saw Cora running after her beloved Labrador. He was uncontrollable and wild, and at that particular moment, Cora was trailing behind to pick up after him.

All in all, it was a welcoming sight.

"Morning!" I called out to them. A chorus of greetings met me as we started our jog on a scenic section of the Meewasin Valley Trail, which winds through the city and up and down the riverbed. Parts of it are populated by dense white spruce and dogwood trees, making it feel like a hidden escape.

The fact that most of Garnet's friends were female wasn't lost on me. He'd worked hard to keep these friendships strong even when it caused problems in his previous marriage. I was noticing that loyalty was very important to him; it came through not just in his long-term friendships but in his commitment to showing up when he said he would for our sessions. I also attributed his preference for female friends to his need for emotional connection. As we'd gotten to know each other, I came to understand that part of this need stemmed from his experiences in childhood, which I'd pieced together based on breadcrumbs Garnet dropped here and there. He didn't like to talk much about his past and particularly disliked any suggestion that he'd had it harder than anyone else. What he did discuss, however, was how he moved past his family's belief system.

Ever since our conversation about habits, I'd become even more curious about how he overcame the dysfunction and abuse he suffered at the hands of his family of origin. His ability to articulate the steps he took to build new habits was so remarkable, and I wondered if he could do the same on this topic.

Overcoming obstacles had been on my mind lately, because I was starting to feel as though I'd hit a wall personally and professionally. My personal training business was successful, but it was plateauing and didn't feel as satisfying to me as it once did. I was getting restless about what was next, but for the first time in my life, I was having a hard time envisioning what that might be. I suspected this might be a brick—one of those inherited, limiting beliefs about what I could accomplish in life —but I wasn't sure how to remove it.

I'd been jogging up ahead with Moira, but I slowed down until I was keeping pace with Garnet.

"Garnet," I said, "I have a question for you."

"Shoot," he said.

"I'm trying to figure out how to take my business to the next level, but every time I try to envision what's next, I come up with nothing. How have you pictured what you want your life to look like when you're feeling stuck? Is it deliberate, or does change just happen organically?"

"It was deliberate, and I know exactly what it was," he said. "Dreaming."

This was not what I expected. "Like, dreams at night?" I asked.

"No, daydreams."

"Say more."

"Well, when I was a kid, I used to read *The Hardy Boys* books. My nurses in the hospital—I'll never forget their kindness. They always made sure I had books to read, and that's where I saw a picture of how life could be: a loving family, enough money to have the things you need and some of the things you want. I used to dream, very clearly, of having those things myself, and it was what kept me going. As a kid, I had a very specific dream: I dreamt I would have $100,000 and a swimming pool that my friends could come swim in. In other words, I wanted to be wealthy. Coming from a very poor family, this was outside anything I'd ever experienced. Now I know that I was manifesting an outcome in my mind."

I was surprised. Without realizing it, Garnet was talking about a technique known in sports psychology as visualization. The practice involves imagining a future outcome in specific detail using all five senses—sight, smell, taste, touch, and hearing. The brain doesn't know the difference between taking an action and imagining it, and it's a powerful tool for creating pathways to success. It's something I use with elite athletes.

"Dreams trigger goals," Garnet continued. "They give us a picture of a different future and supply us with the energy to move toward it."

"But how did you hold onto those dreams? How did you keep them from slipping away?"

"Dreams start as burning desires, and those are divine gifts. No one knows how or why we're given these gifts, but if we nurture them, they will come into existence. They will also become a driving force and a compass in your life."

I'd asked the question about breaking through my mental barriers with the assumption that Garnet would offer up "The Five Habits to Pivoting in Business" or some other CEO-ish, hard-boiled advice. Dreaming felt too ephemeral at first, almost like a waste of time.

Daydreaming is exactly what we tell kids *not* to do at school. But as we jogged along, the idea began to take root, in part because as soon as he mentioned "burning desire," I realized I was already implementing this idea in another area of my life.

Unbeknownst to Garnet at that time, my burning desire had always been to own horses. From a young age, I've wanted to be around them as much as possible. It wasn't a desire I could trace back to anything; just like Garnet said, it was as if the desire was placed in me by the grace of the universe. When I was 11, a woman who owned a local barn let me come after school every day to care for the animals in exchange for riding lessons. It was the happiest I'd ever been; I can still recall the euphoria rising up in my chest when I opened the gates and smelled the hay, heard the horses whinnying, saw the other riders out in the field.

For most of my adult life, I didn't have enough money to lease a horse, let alone buy one.

I also didn't have the time to take care of one. But recently, I'd allowed myself to revisit that passion. I wasn't sure what had prompted it; maybe it was the feeling of dissatisfaction in my job or a desire to expand my life beyond family and work. But as soon as I permitted the thought to enter my mind, as soon as I stopped myself from judging it and allowed the desire to exist in my brain and body unchallenged, it was like opening a Pandora's box. That burning desire was relit, and I held that image clearly in my mind—vividly, using all five senses—to keep myself focused on the goal of incorporating horses into my life in whatever way possible. I could once again smell the hay from the barn; see the animals' brown, white, and black coats; feel their silky manes.

I was surprised to realize that I'd also been using this technique of visualization, one that I'd studied and used with elite athletes, without consciously naming what I was doing. If I could use it to incorporate my passion back into my life, why couldn't I use it to imagine the next steps of my business?

"I can't believe I haven't put this together myself yet," I said to Garnet. "I really believe in visualization. I just hadn't thought about using it in this particular way."

"Well, sometimes we need to hear things from other people in order for them to click into place," he said.

"When I teach visualization, I tell clients that one of the keys is repetition—doing it over and over again," I said. "That makes it easier to travel back to it. It's a very powerful tool."

"It's one of the most fundamental elements of how I moved past my family's belief systems," said Garnet. "As I've gotten older, something else I've learned is that people who don't dream, or don't allow their dreams to blossom, become bitter and resentful later in life."

"I've seen that too," I said. "Choosing not to go forward with a dream is choosing to allow something to die. I believe it causes physical, psychological, and spiritual sickness because you're repressing something that was divinely determined to be expressed through you. You have to keep feeding and nurturing a dream."

"That's right. Another pitfall I've seen is people letting their current reality influence their dreams," said Garnet. "They tell themselves they can't do or be or have something because they can't see it in their day-to-day life. But that's exactly the point: dreams are meant to expand your existing environment. In fact, I *still* dream."

"What are some of your dreams now?"

"I'm going to be a billionaire."

"Why?"

"Well, then I can help more people and make more of a difference in society."

"Help people how?"

"I do a lot to help people now, with health issues and business problems. I could help even more and solve bigger problems."

"It's just surprising to hear someone say that out loud."

"I'm telling you because saying it out loud is part of making it a reality and holding myself accountable. Want to try?"

"Okay..." I began. I thought of my old barn and how much I wanted to be back in that space. "This might surprise you, but my dream is to own horses and a ranch."

Garnet didn't miss a beat. "What color would that ranch be?"

"White," I said, without even thinking.

"And how many horses would you have?"

"Seven," I said, chuckling at the thought, although I knew what he was doing and I appreciated it. In order for dreams or visualizations to work, they needed to have as much detail as possible.

After the run, I was anxious to get back home. My conversation with Garnet had lit a fire in me to use the power of visualization to dream up my next step. I knew the first step: find a quiet place and let my mind wander. When I got home, I changed into comfortable clothing and sat on the couch. My partner had taken our son out for the day, so it was unusually calm. I closed my eyes, took a deep breath, and began to dream.

Things to Think On
Learning to Dream Big

Dreams are one of the first steps we can take towards building a better future for ourselves. If we can't see what we want in our mind, we can't set goals to reach it. It could be called dreaming, though it could also be called visualization.

Visualization is the practice of imagining the outcome we want in very specific detail, using all five senses. By doing this, we can start to imagine a new future for ourselves. It's important to note that visualization should be positive imagery, not a tool for beating ourselves up. It's not about thinking of what we haven't done yet or comparing ourselves to what we see on social media. It's about finding our core truth and desires—what the *real* us wants—and letting our imagination do the work without worrying about the "how": *How will I accomplish this?* Instead, we can just let our minds paint a vivid picture of the end result.

Visualization Exercises

If this feels unfamiliar, there are exercises we can do to put us in a better space to start visualizing what we want or dreaming of the life we want to live. The examples below aren't definitive or all-encompassing, but they can be a good place to start:

1. Imagine a place you went when you were very young, such as a park that your parents took you to or a grassy area. Close your eyes and go sit in the center of that place, and answer the following questions:

- What can you see just in front of you?
- Is it sunny today, or rainy, or cloudy? What's the weather like?
- Can you feel that weather on your skin? How does it feel?
- Are there any smells that are coming to you as you're sitting here?
- Can you hear anything?
- How do you feel right now?

The purpose of this exercise is to remember that every experience is a multi-sensory experience. We can smell things, hear things, see things, and they don't have to be in our physical reality. We can live in any moment in our mind through visualization, and we have complete control over anything that might happen in that moment. We could decide that it's going to rain, or that the flowers are going to bloom. Our mind doesn't know if it's really happening or we're simply dreaming it up.

2. Use this exercise to paint a highly vivid picture of where you

want to be in the future. This will be something you've never seen in real life but that you know you want. For anyone who is a student, imagine walking across the stage to get your diploma. What will you be wearing? What will the auditorium smell like? Who will be in the audience? What will the dean's hand feel like when you shake it?

Another example: Imagine you want to build a race car. What parts do you see laid out in front of you? Will you build it for dirt or pavement? What color will it be? Where are you when you're building it, and what does it feel like to be in that space? Let your imagination wander wherever it wants to go; there are no wrong dreams.

Discovering What We Want

For some of us, identifying our desires is the very first step. We either haven't been encouraged to think about our wants and passions this way or we've been actively *dis*couraged from thinking about it. This is a simple and straightforward exercise, but it can help us investigate and discover our burning desires. We can ask ourselves the following questions and allow the answers to bubble up through our mind, with no judgment as they emerge:

1. What do I love to do?
2. If there were no barriers to doing that thing, how would my life be different?

In the second question, "barriers" refers to anything standing in our way: money, people around us who don't believe in this line of inquiry, where we live, or what we currently do for work. We can allow our minds to drift to that place of possibility, where there are no limitations and anything could happen.

I arrived in Canada as a hopeful 16-year-old, dreaming that the move would eradicate my problems and maybe even my entire past. My father lived in a beautiful city in British Columbia called Kelowna. His new wife was well-off, and their house was a sprawling ranch. I was given a room over the garage that afforded me privacy but also a deep sense that I wasn't part of the family home.

Regardless, my teenage self was gob-smacked by their lifestyle, which I perceived as a combination of money and North American affluence; very different from Europeans with similar means. Coming from a home where I was accustomed to hot water running only between the hours of 7 and 8 a.m., I'd never encountered anything like free-flowing hot water before.

But I quickly discovered that things weren't going to go as smoothly as I'd hoped.

My first hurdle was qualifying to apply to university, which was my most pressing and immediate goal. Because students in the U.K. graduate one year younger than students in Canada, admissions officials didn't know what to do with me or my foreign transcript. My father and I spent months calling around to colleges for advice, and finally, it was decided I should complete the core classes for Canadian 12th-graders: math, physics, chemistry, and biology. I enrolled in a nighttime adult education program and based on the strength of my exams and academics, I was accepted to the University of Saskatchewan in Saskatoon.

The school was 800 miles from where my father and stepmother lived, and an acquaintance of theirs helped me find a room to rent in a condo. I flew out to my new home alone, knowing nobody, and with no money in my pockets. I'd worked three jobs during my brief time in Kelowna, though, and came prepared with a resume. On my first day in Saskatoon, I began walking around to stores and restaurants to hand it out. Within a few weeks, I had two part-time jobs.

This turned out to be more fortuitous than I realized, because I quickly discovered that despite my stepmother's wealth, she and my father were not going to reliably cover my expenses. She considered the money to be hers more than my father's, and certainly more than this 16-year-old's whom she'd only just met.

None of this struck me as an odd or unusual way to begin my college years. Because of the way I was raised, knowing that I was on my own after age 16, I assumed I would be expected to make my own way. Even if it had occurred to me to ask for help, I thought that doing so would make me vulnerable. It would expose a truth that I was barely able to admit to myself: that I was a burden and a duty, and that people helped me because it was the right thing to do, not because I was deeply loved and cared for or because people believed in me. This was a painful truth to know, but it did teach me at an early age that I needed to believe in myself.

My initial plan for college was to study at the university's equine veterinary medicine program. I loved horses, spending time outdoors, and caring for animals. But in my freshman year, I learned that the program only accepted 40 students at a time. Most were residents of Saskatchewan, and the majority were applying for the program as a second degree.

Without thinking much about it, I abandoned the idea. I was young enough to simply follow the path that life was laying out for me, and it so happened that I was good at the kinesiology courses I was taking as part of my veterinary prerequisites. I was fascinated by how the body works—I'd always been an athlete, even during my illness—and the coursework came naturally to me.

In my junior year, a teacher guided me through applying for the honors program, and I was accepted. I began working in the school's cardiac rehabilitation facility, and soon after graduation, I got a job in Vancouver, British Columbia as a field consultant for a private multidisciplinary health company that worked to help people on long-term disability return to the workforce. Just like when I moved to Saskatoon for college, I got lucky with finding a place to live in B.C.

In those days, you had to buy listings for rentals; this was pre-internet. I drove around with this list, and the first place I found happened to be a basement suite in Kerrisdale, which I didn't know at the time was one of the wealthiest neighborhoods in the city. While her son was away at college, the woman who posted the listing was renting out his basement suite at a very reduced rate in an effort to do something nice for young people. She liked me enough to take me on, and it was time for my real life to start.

Through small gestures, I was assisted at critical moments in accomplishing what I did.

My father and his wife, while not financially supportive, helped me navigate my way to university. Their friend found me a place to live, my teachers paved the way for me to thrive academically, and then this older woman housed me for a rent I could afford. Still, it would take years for me to consciously realize that others in my life were helping me through their gestures, or that I could open myself up consciously to accepting others' help. At the time, what stood out to me was how alone I felt.

During my time at the University of Saskatchewan, I briefly moved in with an older man. To demonstrate his disapproval, my father did the same thing he'd always done—he disappeared from my life, and from then on, I heard from him only sporadically. For many years after, I struggled deeply with his absence. I always saw it as a choice he made not to be in my life, even though I would've readily welcomed him back into mine.

That second estrangement from my father hurt me, and certainly came as a shock. Still, I never thought at the time that it would be so final.

4. Values Are the Core of a Prosperous Life

"You, who are on the road
Must have a code you try to live by..."

—*"Teach Your Children," Crosby, Stills, Nash & Young*

Date: January 5, 2012
Time: 5 a.m.
Session: 50

January came around so fast I felt like I had whiplash. This time of year was always busy for me; my clients tended to cancel training sessions during the holidays, then re-up their fitness goals on January 1. It meant I usually had a good month financially and a challenging month personally—I was so busy with work that I wasn't able to spend as much time with my family as I would have liked.

This time around, that strain on my schedule also left me

with almost no time to think about pivoting my business, so I put it on the back burner temporarily.

The morning of my first session with Garnet in the new year, I knew he was operating on almost no sleep. He'd been traveling throughout the holidays and had just returned from a business trip. He texted me the previous day to let me know that he still wanted to meet despite having landed back in Saskatoon at midnight the night before. As always, when I arrived at his building, he was freshly showered and shaved, dressed in his workout gear, and ready to go.

"Morning," he said as I walked through the doors.

"Good morning," I said. I knew he was trying to sound cheerful, but at that moment, I could tell he was exhausted. As he turned towards the door to start our run, I decided to change course. I knew from experience that sometimes what a client really needed was rest. But clients like Garnet, who tended to push through pain rather than worry about injury, were usually the least likely to take it. In fact, I knew it probably would have felt easier for Garnet to bolt out the door and mentally check out for a long run than to do what I was asking him to do: slow down, focus, and shore up weaknesses in training.

"We're going to stay inside today," I said, steering him away from the door.

We doubled back and headed for the gym, which was occupied at that time by only one other brave soul willing to face down the morning darkness. I grabbed a mat and some bands. Garnet had been struggling with a tight calf muscle, so I decided we could use this day as a recovery session. When I told him that, he bristled.

"Isn't it more important to work on distance?" said Garnet. We'd decided to do Kananaskis, the 100-mile relay in Alberta, and he was eager to work up to the full length of the leg he'd be taking.

"It is, but it's more important to remember the need for cross-training, corrective exercise, and self-care. My most important role as a coach is not just to encourage and support you when things get tough, but to ask you to take a break."

As we worked through his stretches, Garnet asked about my holidays and how the new year was shaping up.

"It's busier than ever," I said, "which is great news. My existing clients are referring me out, so I have back-to-back sessions almost every day."

"That's wonderful," he said. "And what are you doing to move toward your goal of pivoting the business?"

My stomach flipped. I felt like I'd been called on in class without having read the assignment. "It's on the back burner for now," I said.

Garnet stopped mid-stretch and turned to look at me. "Why?"

"I'm just too busy. I need to keep generating income. My job has more earning potential than my partner's, so I need to take whatever opportunities come my way." I hoped I sounded business-like and certain.

Garnet sat up. "If you don't mind me asking, Olivia, how old are you?"

"I don't mind. I'm thirty-two."

He nodded. "My business crisis came when I was just a little older, at forty. That was when I lost everything. And if I look back at that time, before I was forty and after, the difference was that I had a great consultant who taught me how to focus on values."

"I think I know what my values are," I said.

"That's good, but the question is, are you living by them? Your core values are the essence of your life—who you are before you think. When you understand and name them, it gives you a base from which to function."

"Okay, so what are your core values?"

"Most people have five or six, and I can tell you that my top two are honesty and integrity."

"Why those two?"

"Well, honesty is because you must do what you say you're going to do. I can't look myself in the mirror in the morning if I'm not living that way. So that's a no-brainer."

"What about integrity?"

"It aligns with honesty. It's a sense of personal responsibility, which ties into my commitment to things like being punctual and circling back with people. I do these things even when they're not convenient for me, even if it causes me discomfort or messes with my day."

"I *have* seen you operate that way with your friends. And what's unusual about it is that you invest the emotional energy of thinking through the most ethical and honest approach to a given situation, and how to do it without burdening other people. It reminds me of the Brené Brown quote, 'Integrity is choosing courage over comfort; choosing what is right over what is fun, fast, or easy; and choosing to practice our values rather than simply professing them.'"

"That about sums it up!"

We moved from the bands to the wall and began working on stretching Garnet's calf.

Kananaskis was six months away, but I worried that if we didn't keep up his bodily awareness, balance, and active range of motion, he would not be ready for such a long distance run. As we did so, a question occurred to me.

"Here's something I'm curious about," I said. "What happens for you if you *don't* live in alignment with your values? If you stretch the truth or avoid a difficult interaction even though you know it's the right one?"

"I feel physically sick, like an utter failure. There's no two ways about it. The good news is that there's a way to move past it, although it isn't easy."

"What's that?"

"Analyze why you did it and own up to it," said Garnet. "Plain and simple. So if I told you a white lie to protect your feelings, for example, that's still a lie. I would work and work and work to understand why I did that, and then one day I would tell you, 'I said this thing and it really wasn't what I meant.' That doesn't make it right, but you have to try to straighten the ship."

"What you're describing is very difficult for most people to do," I said. "Looking in the mirror and being honest with ourselves is one of the hardest things we can attempt."

"No one said it was easy." *Ouch*. Garnet had a way of putting things, I was beginning to realize, that could sting a bit.

"Well, one of my core values is excellence. I try to show up for everyone as my absolute best self. So when I have all these clients, it's hard not to take the extra time to do my best for them."

"What are some others?"

"I would say...connection, courage, compassion, challenge, and learning."

"Great. Do you apply all of those values, including excellence, in all areas of your life?"

I thought about that month and how little time I'd spent with my son and partner, the difficulty I was having balancing work and family, and how I always seemed to land on the side of doing too much work.

"I try," I said. I knew it sounded defensive.

"I know you do," Garnet said. "But if we don't figure it out —how to live within and in alignment with our values—we will regret it later in life."

It reminded me of our conversation around bricks. What I

noticed, if I slowed the whole thing down, was that my limiting beliefs sometimes got in the way of living in alignment with my values. When I tried to balance my work and life more evenly, I immediately ran into an old belief that told me I was lazy for not working myself to the bone. The result was that I wasn't as present and available as I wanted to be as a partner and mother.

"Okay," I said, "but using your values as a compass to guide you in life is—at least I think—a very high level of living. So how the hell do you do it?"

"One of the most important elements is not worrying about what other people think about you. You can only worry about what *you* think about you. If you understand your values, when you wake up in the morning, you say, 'Am I true to them?' And if you are, the rest of the world can shove off."

My mind was a little bit blown. Garnet often put these ideas in ways that seemed so straightforward, even though I knew they required a lot of work. It was as if he could distill the things he'd learned so far in life into their purest essence.

"It seems like that would also help you deal with failure," I said. "Because if you tried something and it didn't work out, as long as you knew you did it your way and you were true to yourself, that would give you the faith to keep going."

"Exactly. So, with that being said, if you're being the best Olivia you can be—then you're selling yourself short by staying stagnant with your business. What would it take for you to move forward with that?"

The truth was that I didn't really know.

"We could simplify your business idea down to three flash-cards, Olivia," Garnet continued as we cooled down in the lobby of his building.

"Oh really?"

"Yes. There are three things that hold everyone back, and they're the same for almost all of us, because it's all human nature. It's shame, guilt, and fear. If you simply said, 'I'm going to give you these three cards, and I want you to lay them on the table in the order in which you think they affect you the most. My job is to help you overcome all of those things,' people could relate to that."

"I agree that the message needs to be simplified. I have the sense that my inability to take the time to sit down and reflect on those things is holding me back in some way; maybe like, in a significant way."

"I'll be very candid. I think when the right time comes to do it, you will."

As I drove home, I thought about all the things I wanted to do if only I had the time.

I hadn't told most of my clients, but over the course of the past few years, I'd become disenchanted with the fitness industry. In the early years of my personal training business, people came to me with the clear goal of changing the size and shape of their body. At that time, I colluded with that narrative. It was the dominant cultural belief system—that health necessarily meant weight loss—and since exercise was so helpful for me to feel confident and safe in my body, I thought I could offer that agency to other people at the same time as we worked towards their more aesthetic goals.

But after several years in the industry, with fitness still so laden with a weight-based approach, I felt I wasn't serving my clients on the level I wanted to. I knew I had all the knowledge and skills, but I still couldn't help people achieve the types of body transformation journeys that were being propagated on reality TV shows, celebrity magazines, and women's magazines.

No matter how much their lives improved through regular exercise, my clients felt like they failed if they hadn't lost weight. They would say, "I'm feeling better, I have more energy, but it just doesn't seem to be working—the number on the scale hasn't changed." I started to realize that if we as a society didn't unpack the social conditioning around our bodies, people—often women—wouldn't be able to relieve themselves of the burden of feeling uncomfortable in their own skin.

I wanted to counter the idea that all of life's problems could be solved through diet and exercise—that if only my clients lost 10 or 15 pounds, they'd be happy and at peace. Instead, I wanted to instill a sense that healthy eating and consistent movement were good *for their own sake*, because they helped us feel our best and do our best in the world.

This, at its core, was how I hoped to pivot my business. I was excited just thinking about it, since one of my other core values was learning, I wanted to take clients on a learning journey with me. I noticed how energized I felt when I thought about it, in contrast to the occasional dread I felt at the thought of back-to-back training sessions.

I knew Garnet was onto something. The question was: what did I have to do next?

Things to Think On
Identifying and Living by Our Core Values

Without identifying our core values, it becomes impossible to live our life in alignment with our truest, highest self. However, it's important to differentiate between values, human needs, and social conditioning.

All human beings have ways of operating that serve to get our needs met. For instance, we may tell a lie to protect ourselves from overly harsh punishment that would come if we told the truth. Or, we may have been socialized to prioritize our appearance when in reality, it's something that doesn't really resonate with who we are at our core.

With that said, core values are about *meaning*: What makes our life truly worthwhile and energizing?

We've included a long list of possible values that might resonate. The list includes a wide range of feelings, experiences, lifestyles, and characteristics, such as serenity, wealth, spirituality, teamwork, joy, collaboration, and kindness. While reading through a list of values and deciding which ones resonate most, it's important to notice how our bodies feel and how we respond to the words. Are some things non-negotiable? Are others not as important? By doing this, it can become a lesson in getting to know ourselves. As we do so, we get to know how we want to exist in the world: what matters to us and what defines the person we want to be.

To refine this even further, we can take a pen or pencil and leave a mark next to each word, indicating how important it is to us with the following numbering system (while remembering that there are no right or wrong answers):

1—Not important to me
2—Somewhat important to me
3—Important to me
4—Very important to me
5—The most important to me

List of Values

As you number each value, you'll begin to see certain words rise to the top as others fall to the bottom. Try repeating the exercise a few times, even on different days or weeks, and see if you get the same answers. Eventually, you should end up with five to eight core values.

- Acceptance
- Accomplishment
- Accord
- Accountability
- Acknowledgement
- Admiration
- Allegiance
- Authenticity
- Authority
- Beauty
- Capability

- Caring
- Community
- Cooperation
- Courage
- Creativity
- Determination
- Dignity
- Discipline
- Diversity
- Duty
- Earnestness
- Education
- Efficacy
- Empathy
- Exploration
- Faith
- Family
- Financial stability
- Fitting in
- Flexibility
- Freedom
- Friendship
- Frugality
- Generosity
- Governance
- Grit
- Growth
- Honesty
- Hope
- Humility
- Humor
- Inclusion
- Independence

- Influence
- Information
- Ingenuity
- Inquisitiveness
- Integrity
- Job security
- Joy
- Justice
- Love
- Minimalism
- Morals
- Nature
- Occupation
- Openness
- Patience
- Patriotism
- Peace
- Philanthropy
- Quality
- Reciprocity
- Relaxation
- Reliability
- Responsibility
- Risk-taking
- Safety
- Satisfaction
- Self-actualization
- Self-assurance
- Self-expression
- Spirituality
- Sportsmanship
- Stability
- Thankfulness

- Thoughtfulness
- Tradition
- Travel
- Trust
- Vision
- Vulnerability
- Wealth
- Well-being
- Wellness
- Wisdom

After buying and selling my first hotel, my business took off beyond anything I could have fathomed as I made my first million and then multiplied it dozens of times over. I poured myself into my business, working open to close, seven days a week. In the middle of it, I got married, had two children and made every attempt to be home for dinner to read to my daughters. Though things were going well, I worried that I might one day regret how much time I spent working instead of with my family.

Nevertheless, my hard work was paying off, and for the next decades, I continued to build wealth in my hotel and real estate businesses. In my late thirties, however, things began to falter. I lost one hotel, and then another, mostly due to too high a dose of optimism coupled with rampant stupidity and bad management.

For example, I had one hotel in an urban area that I sold, but the buyer defaulted so I took the hotel back, but by that time, it was in rough shape. I thought I could turn things around if I acquired some smaller hotels that could operate at a profit. But I made bad management hires—including hiring members of my own family—and the hotels performed below my optimistic expectations. Those were fixable problems, to my mind; they were still small.

To ensure I fed my family and cut costs, I started working at my hotels, long shifts, and selling life insurance on the side. But then things started to snowball, and I found myself working 20 hours per day Mondays through Fridays and 14 hours on Saturdays and eight hours on Sundays. It wasn't sustainable and it didn't make it profitable (or healthy for my family). I ended up losing the hotels one by one until finally they were all gone and suppliers were coming to me saying they hadn't been paid.

Just like that, what had once been a multi-million-dollar business came crumbling down.

Around the same time, I enrolled in a program called Strategic Coach®, led by Dan Sullivan. The program met for one day every quarter, in small groups, workshops, and lectures. I signed up because I'd started selling life insurance to bolster my income and had heard that Strategic Coach® would be a good way to scale my business—lots of other agents were attending, and I'd just qualified to join financially.

What I didn't know at the time was that Strategic Coach® wouldn't just teach me more about money. Instead, it would change my life in every conceivable way.

At the time, I was a chain smoker who weighed over 300 pounds, worked around the clock, and lived recklessly. In one year, I got 26 speeding tickets. Though it took me time to realize it, my lifestyle was part of the reason my business had fallen apart. All the different parts of my life fed into one another, and I couldn't be successful in one area while letting all the other areas deteriorate.

My mind opened to this reality early on, after attending one of Strategic Coach's® initial activities where participants were asked to write down the "messes" in their lives and to figure out strategies to clean them all up. As I began that task, something shifted inside me. I realized I could never turn my business around without turning my personal life around. One didn't exist without the other. The problems in my personal life were holding me back from further success in my professional life and vice versa.

I began making a list of all the things I needed to change, which included aspects of my health, finances, and relationships. I approached this as if I were in a quiet room by myself admitting to all of my mistakes—even, and maybe especially, those that caused me the most shame.

In addition to moving towards a healthier lifestyle, another major discovery through Strategic Coach® was that declaring bankruptcy was my best option, which I hadn't considered. After losing my hotels, I'd paid off all the mom-and-pop suppliers to whom I still owed money, because I didn't want to let them down. Eventually, the outstanding debts I had left were to the government. It was a loan I could have worked through, but I would have struggled endlessly to do so, and it would have come at the cost of greatly slowing down my progress. Though I'd been convinced that it was the best way forward, making the choice to declare bankruptcy was a massive hit to my ego and my pride. Fighting off the shame of that decision was one of the most difficult parts of my early journey.

As I learned firsthand, nobody knew humility until they were standing in front of another man—a judge—and telling him that they'd failed at business and had no money left. But through that painful process, I was starting to learn an important lesson: none of the goals I had for my life would ever be easy to attain.

My sister Cassie was two years older than me, and she was also brilliant. She devoured books, wrote poetry and essays, and excelled in all the arts. But ever since I could remember, she struggled with severe emotional problems. She ran away from home many times and always displayed erratic behavior. It was one of the reasons I felt it was my job to be the put-together one, the one who didn't cause any problems.

In the 1990s, though, neither of us got the care we needed. She attempted suicide several times and was in and out of psychiatric care, but never with any tools or medications that helped her to stabilize.

As Cassie got older, she had a very hard time finding her way in the world despite her academic achievements. She tried college but was consumed with finding a boyfriend. She tried nursing and business school but was often derailed due to a life crisis, bad relationship, or lack of enthusiasm for the profession. She fell into a pattern of romanticizing the idea of things then being unbearably disappointed by the reality.

Her final career path was towards becoming an anesthesiologist, and for a brief time, it seemed like she'd finally found her way. She was enthused by the work and had a loving boyfriend, and we all thought things were turning around. But there is a universe of experience inside all of us, and you never really know what's happening in anyone's cosmos.

At the hospital where she worked, they said she must have been taking home small amounts of sedatives over several months, so no one noticed they were missing. Once she finally had enough for a lethal dose, at 22 years old, she injected herself with an overdose that ended her life.

At this point, my father hadn't spoken to me in two years, but he was the one tasked with calling me. When I picked up the phone, I knew almost immediately. I heard it in his voice, I knew it in my bones. She was gone.

5. Generosity: The Good of Giving

"The way you see people is the way you treat them, and the way you treat them is what they become."

—Goethe

Date: February 1, 2012
Time: 9 a.m.
Session: 58

O n a cold but sunny Sunday morning, I was standing in the kitchen making pancakes for my family. Just as I poured the batter into the pan, I heard what sounded like a revving engine outside.

At first, I chalked it up to a biker passing by. But then the sound got closer and closer, until it stopped right in front of my house.

As I realized what was happening, I laughed out loud.

Garnet told me the week before that he'd bought a Harley-

Davidson. I ribbed him about it at first, telling him that it smacked of a midlife crisis. He didn't mind; he loves cars and motorcycles, and nothing could detract from the joy of his new purchase. I mentioned that my son, Keenan, also loved anything with an engine. Even though he was just a little kid, Keenan would surprise me by noticing things. Once, I was swapping out my summer tires for my winter tires, a chore that I found annoying at best—but Keenan was fascinated by it.

Garnet has two adult daughters, in whom he instilled a love of vehicles, and his eyes lit up when I mentioned Keenan's interest.

"Do you think he'd like to see the motorcycle?" he said.

"I'm sure he'd love it," I replied.

I didn't expect anything to come from it. I often had conversations like this with clients, riffing on potential plans that never saw the light of day. But Garnet was different. His word was his bond. Perhaps more importantly, though, something I'd recently told Garnet about Keenan struck a deep chord in him, which was that Keenan was born with a very rare heart condition that caused him to struggle to catch his breath whenever he engaged in physical activity. I'd known about the condition since before he was born, but our treatment plan was ramping up because we'd just learned that his risk for a heart blockage was increasing. He was now scheduled to get a pacemaker, a massively invasive surgery for a young child. He'd also be evaluated for a corrective procedure that had the potential to fix the difference he was born with.

Garnet related to what Keenan was going through on a primal level. Keenan wasn't able to play sports or run around freely like other kids, and Garnet had experienced something similar because of his asthma. It was a deeply painful childhood memory, and he worried that Keenan would suffer in the same way.

That Sunday, it was all I could do to prevent Keenan from running straight out into the street to see the bike. Before I knew it, Garnet was showing him the engine, the handlebars, the way the motorcycle worked as a piece of machinery. Keenan was enraptured; he asked a million questions, and Garnet seemed to have infinite patience for them.

I knew what was coming.

"Keenan, would you like to take a ride on it?" Garnet said. "If it's okay with your mom and dad, of course."

Keenan turned to me and begged. "Please let me go! I'll be careful!"

We live in an agricultural region; there's a joke about it being so flat that you can see the horizon from another state over. I made them promise to go slowly, and Garnet said he would just take him around the block. I yelled inside to Keenan's dad to make sure it was all right with him, too.

"It'll be good for him," my partner replied. "I wish I could go!"

We helped Keenan strap on his helmet and climb onto the bike. Seeing them together made me happy. Keenan's face was full of joy and wonder, and Garnet's face was full of a surprising goofiness and warmth. I watched as they pulled away, drove slowly down the block, and returned from the other direction moments later.

"How was it?" I asked Keenan.

"Awesome!" he said.

Garnet smiled. "He's a great navigator," he said, and Keenan beamed.

I invited Garnet in for pancakes—I'd made way too many—but he demurred and left, like a fairy godfather.

At our session the next week, I thanked him profusely. Keenan hadn't stopped talking about his ride on the motorcycle all week.

"That was so generous of you to come all the way over just to give him a ride," I said.

"It was my pleasure," he said. "There are a lot of things from my family of origin that I had to overcome, but when it came to generosity, I learned from my father."

Garnet proceeded to tell me that some of his fondest early memories were of Saturdays spent canvassing for the church with his dad. His father did the work on a volunteer basis because he believed in creating community and being available as a resource to people in need. Motivated by compassion, empathy, and kindness, he instilled in Garnet a positive and uplifting association with generosity.

"People were attracted to him because they knew he cared about them," Garnet said. "I admired him so much for that work, and I strive to be like him in that way."

"Well, I can't tell you how much Keenan appreciated you coming over with the bike," I said.

"Does he know that his mother is just as generous?"

The compliment made me self-conscious and bashful. Sometimes Garnet knew how to cut straight to my heart.

"I don't know," I said. "I don't think of myself as unusually generous."

"You know, sometimes I think you don't realize how much you've given me over these past five months," Garnet said. "When we began our work together, I would be dripping sweat five minutes into a workout. Now, I can run five miles and feel fantastic at the end. I know I'm not so easy to work with all the time. I reached these goals because you never gave up on me. In fact, you're saying that I'm generous, but I'm curious: how are *you* able to be so generous and open to seeing the best in people?"

"Well...I suppose one of my beliefs is that generosity is critical to feeling good about ourselves. Helping other people increases our own wellbeing, and that means it generates positive energy that goes out into the world. And it doesn't even have to go both ways. If I assume the best about you, you may or may not reciprocate that feeling, but I've put that positivity into the universe, which is a net gain."

"I agree. It's the butterfly effect."

"Yes!"

"My only caveat to that belief is that you have to be discerning. If someone takes advantage of your generosity, it's critical to set a clear boundary with that person."

"I struggle with that sometimes."

"I used to struggle with it, too. It's a big reason why I lost all the hotels. I kept hiring people because I felt bad for them, and then I kept them around even after they'd shown me who they really were."

Our conversation reminded me of recent work that I'd been doing on self-compassion. The core of the practice was to accept ourselves wherever we currently were in our journey of growth or healing, rather than saying we would accept ourselves once we reached a certain goal. According to those teachings, that foundation was key to setting boundaries and being generous in ways that made sense given the reality of our situation.

"You know, Olivia, this conversation makes me think of a practice that I want to start doing again," said Garnet. "I pick three acts of generosity to do each day, and write them down once they're done. One of my favorites is to look for the good in people and let them know what I see. For example, I used to go into this Starbucks, and I always saw the same barista. I'd always tell her she was doing a great job. One day, I realized something from the loudness of her voice and her mannerisms. She had ADHD, which I knew because I have it, too."

Garnet had mentioned his diagnosis to me before, but only

in passing. I knew he'd gotten his diagnosis later in life, and that it changed the way he viewed himself and his interactions with the world.

"Did you ever mention it to her?" I asked.

"I did. I said, 'Do you know that you have ADHD?' She looked at me kind of funny, but the next time I saw her, she said, '*Garnet!*'—she always greeted me like that—'You were right! I went to the clinic and got an assessment. I do have ADHD! It explains so much!'"

"That's amazing! That must have been life-changing for her."

"It's an example of what simple acts of generosity can do."

Over the next few months, Garnet continued to take Keenan out for special adventures, like going to the John Deere dealership or taking more rides on the motorcycle. Later, Garnet told me that when he first met Keenan, he'd experienced "the most incredible feeling of déjà vu." Part of the reason he came by with the bike in the first place, he explained, was to establish a relationship with Keenan that would let him know that as he got older, someone would always be in his corner—even if that someone was, as Garnet said, "just an old guy." Just as the nurses at the hospital had shown him kindness, he wanted to show kindness to my son. It was one of the most genuine displays of generosity I'd seen from Garnet (though over the years, I would see many more of them).

Seeing how Garnet was with Keenan made me realize that Garnet really didn't do things halfway—he was always all or nothing. It seemed to give him just as much joy as it gave Keenan to think of a plan that would generate extreme joy and an overflow of emotion. Each time Garnet would tell Keenan about his plans for their next adventure, I could see an equal amount of glee on both of their faces. The more I thought about it, the more I realized how important it was—Garnet's generosity towards Keenan, but also how I manifested generosity in my own life in general.

I always tried to be generous with my clients and my family, but I also caught myself walking around with my head down the rest of the time. As I mulled it over, I began to think of little things I could start doing to bring a smile to someone's face—complimenting their work, their outfit, their kids. It was so easy. All I had to do was become aware of it.

Things to Think On
Strengthening Our Capacity
for Generosity

Generosity is about paying things forward—being kind or doing kind things for others without the expectation of them doing anything for us in return. In that regard, it's also part of integrity and doing what needs to be done, even if it comes at an inconvenience to us.

Since it can be such a broad topic, considering specific ideas and principles that play into generosity help us learn to practice it:

1. Generosity doesn't necessarily mean giving money.

Being generous means giving in ways that are available to us. That could mean giving a compliment to the barista we see every day at our local coffee shop or going out of our way to return something we saw someone drop. These things take very little time and effort, but they can turn other people's days around.

2. Think of three or four ways to be generous each day.

Just as it helps with tracking our habits, we should write down our ideas about how we intend to be generous. That way, we can check them off when we've done them each day. By doing this, generosity will become another of our habits.

3. We should show the same generosity to ourselves that we show to others.

As the saying goes, it's important for us to put our own oxygen masks on first. Are we implementing good habits and living by our values? Are we taking care of our physical and mental health? Only then can we truly show up for others.

4. Generosity is lifelong work.

Like all good habits, generosity is a practice. Sometimes it will drop off our radar, but it's easy to pick it back up again by simply returning to our "home base" of writing down our ideas and implementing them.

As I continued to work the plan I'd started at Strategic Coach®, I opened my mind to another idea that would change my life: the possibility of being coachable. My plan necessitated the input of professionals, ranging from doctors to psychiatrists to healers and more. So, for the first time in my life, I began reaching out to others and asking for help.

One of the first people I hired was a consultant, Willy Fornier, who helped me tremendously to refocus on my values and mission. I put in many hours figuring out what mattered most to me in business and in life, and the resulting beliefs allowed me to orient myself each and every day thereafter. In turn, I was able to draft a mission: to help as many people as possible, and to be the best available resource to business owners seeking to optimize their net worth.

However, that notion of being the best didn't mean reaching a goal and then sitting back and relaxing. It meant constantly evolving and innovating, being the best I could be today, not yesterday and not tomorrow.

The concept of focusing on the present was also informed by a counselor I worked with who worked from a Buddhist perspective. She introduced me to literature that pushed me to understand myself on a deeper level, to grapple with my problems on an ongoing basis, and to comprehend how I related to others. Influenced by books such as Going to Pieces Without Falling Apart by Mark Epstein, PhD; The Art of Happiness by the 14th Dalai Lama and Howard Cutler and How to See Yourself as You Really Are by the 14th Dalai Lama, my mindset slowly pivoted to allow for an understanding that change was possible at the deepest level of self.

Of course, "becoming coachable" is the cleaned-up version of how I saw this process in hindsight. The way I usually thought of it was that I had already gotten beat up once, so I wasn't so sure I was smart anymore. By following that thought, the result was that I was able to evolve—basically, from scratch.

During all these changes, I was still determined to support my family. I'd originally gotten into the life insurance business out of necessity, but like my first job at the Bank of Commerce, I quickly discovered that I had an innate aptitude for it. As I built the business that would become The Targeted Strategies Group (TTSG), the largest and most sophisticated insurance brokerage in Canada, which works with high-net-worth individuals and families on insurance and estate planning, I remained focused on utilizing the best practices I'd been learning, personally and professionally. It wasn't a pill, and it wasn't a quick fix. But it was the only way back up.

The convention center in Phoenix, Arizona was full of people I'd admired for years: experienced, elite digital influencers of health and wellness from all over the world. I was there to pitch the idea for my new business and to learn from the best and the brightest in my field.

There was one woman in particular with whom I'd hoped to connect. She was—and is—very visible and successful, and she specializes in fitness for an over-50 demographic. With a similarly niche population as those I was hoping to target, I thought she may be interested in my idea.

During a networking event, I made my way over to her, introduced myself, and asked if I could pitch her my plan. To my delight, she agreed.

For one minute, she listened intently as I gave my elevator pitch: my history with an eating disorder put me on this path to finding a way to offer fitness to the masses that didn't focus on shame, blame, or guilt, but rather embraced a notion that exercise and wellness do not have to be inextricably linked with a body that changes size.

When I was done, she smiled. "Well, everyone dabbled with dieting and a little eating disorder in their teens, right?" she said. "Thanks, but I don't think it's a big enough pain point on which to run a business successfully."

I smiled back and walked away, but inside I was raging. Before the current opioid crisis, eating disorders were the leading cause of death from mental illness. Decades in the fitness and wellness industries had illuminated to me that many people— women in particular—are so harmed and oppressed by beauty, body, and femininity standards that we're robbed of our mental health, predisposed to unhealthy relationships with food and exercise, and consumed by thoughts about our bodies that could be used for advancing our career and more.

If all of that wasn't enough of a pain point, I didn't know what was.

6. Goals Are Our Specific Targets for Success

Date: March 2, 2012
Time: 5 a.m.
Session: 75

As winter turned to spring, Garnet and I amped up our training sessions. Kananaskis was in June, and in order to be prepared, we needed to train very specifically. That meant hitting the trails more than strength training and pushing Garnet to run even when he was traveling and adjusting to a new time zone. The good news was that his business was so busy, there were plenty of days when running served as a brain break for him as well as a way to reinvigorate, get his creative juices flowing, and be inspired. By adhering to his health goal, he was actually increasing his performance at work. This was something I reminded him of frequently.

Our meeting that Friday was the fifth time in a row we'd seen each other, which was very unusual. Usually, Garnet traveled for work at least once a week. This increase in our schedule was good timing for me, because I'd finally turned my attention to pivoting my business, with Garnet giving me advice along the way. After thinking it all over, I'd identified the big picture ways in which I wanted things to change.

Though fitness had morphed into wellness culture, that change had created a situation in which the everyday person never fully knew, even in their own psyche, whether they were pursuing health or simply weight loss. For me, it was no longer enough to simply not collude with that mindset. If I wasn't actively working to undo the body shame and harm created by the culture, then I wasn't doing enough; I would still be allowing fitness culture to exist as it was.

With that in mind, I wanted to reshape the landscape of health and wellness culture and create a safe space for learning and growth for my clients. I wanted to find compelling, alternative ways of engaging in fitness as a form of self-development and growth that also helped people unpack their personal narratives of body shame, guilt, and body-based trauma, embracing movement as a form of liberation. In my heart, I believed that was the healthiest approach we could have toward physical movement, the benefits of which research had demonstrated again and again, and I wanted to reach as many people as possible with that message.

Through that reflection, my work with Garnet was always a beacon of light, since he knew what I was trying to do and didn't let me off the hook, which was as nerve-wracking as it was encouraging.

———

The snow was beginning to melt along the Meewasin Valley Trail, causing big puddles of mud that we had to sidestep or jump over. Because of this, our path was largely empty, with most other runners opting for flatter, drier ground.

Garnet wasted no time. "So," he said, "how's business?"

"Good," I said, hoping he might change the subject. No such luck.

"What did you do last night to work towards your goal?"

"Um...made dinner and got my son to bed on time?"

"Very funny. I mean it. You don't get anywhere new in life without goals."

"Yes, but what about the rest of my life? I don't want my goals to come at the expense of spending time with my family."

"Well, you're in a new position. Until very recently, moms didn't have as many choices. So in a sense, you need to forge a new path. One way to keep yourself on track is something you should be doing anyway: make sure your goals are specific."

"I think they are. I want to pivot my business so that I can help people unlearn toxic messages from diet culture."

"That's your idea, but that's not a specific goal. Let me give you an example. From the time I was four or five years old, I wanted to be rich. But I had no idea what 'rich' meant, so I quantified it by saying I wanted to have $100,000 and a swimming pool. Decades later, when I started doing Strategic Coach, I learned how to formalize goal setting and set three-year plans. They were highly specific. So when I decided to lose weight, I said I wanted to go from 300 pounds to 240. When I decided to get in better shape, I had to define what fitness meant to me, so I said I'd be at the level of fitness I wanted to be at when I could do 100 pushups, 100 sit ups and burpees, and run a 10K. So the question you need to ask yourself is, 'Who is Olivia three years from now? What does her day-to-day look like? What is the metric of success?'"

I took a minute to visualize this new Olivia.

"Okay," I said, "I'm doing large-scale public speaking that's aligned with my heart and head, and it's at a national and international level."

"What's large scale? Because that's not quantifiable. So, thirty speeches per year?"

"Yikes."

"Yes! Goals should feel audacious and uncomfortable."

"Okay...so I'm speaking on large stages. Like TED talks. Digital or in-person."

"Right. And then from there, you create a timetable and break those goals down into manageable steps. Oh, and you have to tell people. Stick the goals to the fridge. Tell whoever will listen. They help with the value of honesty because you can't bullshit a goal; you either reach it, or you don't. And guess what? If you aim for thirty speeches a year and you only get to twenty, that's still pretty damn good."

———

When I got home, I took out my phone and made a quick list of where I might like to see myself in the next year or two: more clients, and infusing my sessions with messages of positivity around movement.

In order to make those changes, I imagined I would have to reach out to existing clients as well as networking to recruit some new ones. I didn't want to face Garnet without having specifics to show him, so as I poured myself a cup of tea and sat down at my dining room table, I thought about the numbers. What would constitute real change, but also be realistic and not cause me to burn out?

I transferred my list from my phone to my laptop; I always think better that way. I had dozens of clients at the time, but I could already imagine that not all of them would be on board. I tried to identify the most open-minded people I worked with and typed their names into a blank document. I came up with seven women and three men. If they converted, perhaps each of them would refer someone else to me, which might result in another 10 new clients.

Ten converted clients and 10 new clients in the next year. Specific goals. I closed my laptop, excited to share my plan with Garnet the next time I saw him.

Things to Think On
Setting Specific Goals

G oals are critical to growth and moving past our families' limiting belief systems, but they don't work unless they're specific. We can't talk in general terms about wanting to do something. Instead, we have to assign tangible numbers or steps to our goals so we can track our progress—and, as Jim Collins writes in *Good to Great*, our goals should be big, hairy and audacious.

To be clear: these goals should be so monumental that they would completely change our lives, things that we are almost afraid to write down. As an example, we could think of an annual salary we would like to make but that feels out of reach —*it isn't*. Once written down, that can become our audacious goal.

To do this, we have to begin by working backwards:

1. Define Our Metric of Success: What will our life look like when we've attained our goal? We can use our visualization skills to see and feel it. We should also notice what we experience in our bodies when we see ourselves at that new place in our life.

2. Write It Down: We have to describe our goals in specific detail using numbers, such as dollar amounts and dates. If we're interested in publishing a book, we should write down how many copies we'll sell. If we're interested in building a business, we should write down how many clients we'll get in our first year.

3. Work Backwards: First, we should write down the bold steps we need to take to make progress. Then, we put them on a timeline and set up a system for ourselves to track any incremental progress.

4. Tell Other People: Speaking our goals aloud, *to other people*, serves two purposes: it makes them real for us, and it makes us accountable. It becomes harder to put off our plans once we've already announced them.

I was in Toronto for work when I got the call.

It was a sunny afternoon, and I was in the car driving from one meeting to another when the phone rang. It was my middle sister who delivered the news that at 39, our youngest sister had been found dead from an overdose of pills. Additionally, my middle sister herself had written the prescription that killed her.

During the call, I was passing a financial company I knew of—a small white structure with green trim—whose colors would forever be seared into my mind thereafter. From that moment on, I would always associate them with the news of my youngest sister's suicide.

I pulled my car over in front of that now-sickeningly cheerful building, feeling like I might throw up, but I didn't have time to tend to those emotions. I already knew the burden would fall largely on me to help my family remain on track, as much as they possibly could. Immediately, my mind went into overdrive. How would I get home? What needed to be done? Without even thinking about it, I did what I'd always done: I pushed the pain down as far as it could go and put a tight lid over it.

Soon after, I flew back to my hometown to attempt to pick up the pieces, but it would not be so easily done. After all, it was my family's second funeral in as many months. Just six weeks earlier, my brother, four-and-a-half years younger than I was, had also taken his own life.

My brother's death, although horrific, hadn't surprised me. He had always been wild, still partying at age 30 with a wife and three children. Prior to his suicide, he had been facing penalties from not paying his child support. Even so, he'd been our mother's golden child. I'd tried to help him as things were going swiftly downhill, but I knew that nothing I could've done would have prevented the way things ended. My sister's death, on the other hand, had come from out of the blue.

She'd struggled early in life, having had a difficult time at school and, later, with finding a stable partner. But after dropping out of high school, she went back for her diploma and then for an accounting degree. She was a survivor, always overcoming whatever difficulty was in her way. Even so, she was plagued by pain—stomach pain that made it almost impossible for her to digest food, as well as severe menstrual pain. In the end, I suspected it wasn't just the physical pain that caused her to end her life. I think she blamed herself for our brother's decision to die.

The entire two-month period was an unfathomable shock, like a punch to the head. I remained in touch with my parents as much as possible throughout their ordeal, although it was profoundly painful because there was nothing that could have alleviated their agony. My mother started gambling, losing all the remaining money that she and my father had, and she kept going until she died. My father turned even more strongly to his faith and religion, but he could never recover; it wasn't something that could be resolved. Like many people, my father had lived his life thinking that he could fix a lot of things, but nobody could ever even begin to figure out how to fix what he'd just been through.

Montana's Cookhouse was a Western-themed barbecue spot located just a few blocks from campus. In my last year of college and after graduation, I worked there as a bartender, where I made a handful of good friends. Montana's Cookhouse was also where I met the man who would become Keenan's father.

Our relationship was on-again, off-again for most of the time we were together, but he was a kind person who welcomed me into his life and family almost immediately. During our first Christmas together, he invited me to his parent's house. Being so far from my own family, I was like a lost puppy; anyone who showed me any significant affection was someone I immediately latched onto.

Since our relationship was so bumpy, I thought it would come to an end when I took the field consultant position in Vancouver. But after a few months in British Columbia, I was lonely. I made new friends at my job, but it wasn't enough to stop me from saying yes when he asked if he could move in with me. He'd always wanted to leave Saskatoon—where he was from, and where his family still lived—and my being in Vancouver presented the excuse he needed.

Things did not get better between us when he arrived. For a year and a half, we were still back and forth and up and down. Sometimes we even slept separately. But one day, everything changed.

I'd been feeling sick for a few weeks in the fall, but chalked it up to a cold or allergies since the weather was getting colder faster. But when I didn't feel any better, and suddenly began feeling nauseous in the mornings, I took a pregnancy test.

It came back positive.

To say I was shocked would be an understatement. Since my eating disorder, my menstrual cycles had been completely unpredictable, and in truth, I subconsciously thought I'd messed my body up enough that I might never be able to get pregnant. It *was probably that line of thinking that led me to put myself in a situation where I was risking pregnancy, because I didn't know I had anything to risk.*

My partner wanted me to get an abortion, and I considered it. But I thank the universe for a conversation I had with a coworker one day. She was the mother of three boys, and we were driving to see a client together. She was behind the wheel, and as I explained to her the choice in front of me, she turned to me and said, "Olivia, no one ever regrets having a baby."

Of course, I know that's not completely true, but at the time, it was what I needed to hear. It released me of the shame I felt for having an unplanned pregnancy and the feeling of being a failure for not making my first job a significant step forward in my life. I told my partner, and to his credit, he was supportive.

Together, we forged ahead.

———

The price of daycare came as a shock—almost as much as the pregnancy itself.

After I had Keenan, I took maternity leave for what I thought would be a few months. But the more I looked around, the more discouraged and panicked I became. Most daycares wouldn't accept children younger than a year-and-a-half, and even those still charged nearly $1,500 a month. It was money we didn't have, and so we reluctantly accepted the reality that we would have to move back to Saskatoon to be closer to the only family we had—my partner's parents.

To be clear, they were kind and wonderful people. My partner's mother jumped right in to help, and my partner was a great dad from day one, spending time with Keenan as much as he could and helping with all the parenting tasks. All the same, we couldn't rely on them forever. I wanted—and needed—to get back to work.

The internal drive that rocketed me out of England into Canada, through the Canadian education system, and into a good job in Vancouver, hadn't gone away. I never wanted to be a stay-at-home mom; I was an extrovert who thrived around people. So, after sending out a handful of applications, I got a job with the city as a Programs Manager at the local leisure center facility. It was a great job with steady pay, health insurance, and good benefits, and it would pay a pension if I stayed through retirement. It was the kind of job that some people would have killed for.

The only problem was I wasn't one of those people.

If I didn't already know that I didn't fit into bureaucratic environments, I found out within several months of that city job. I hated the constricting hours, clocking in and clocking out like a robot, feeling like all I had to look forward to were tiny pay increases and the same routine, day in and day out, for the rest of my working life.

As I tried to figure out my next move, I started a side hustle. A woman I knew, a nurse, had opened a small personal training studio nearby, and I began taking clients there. It was the mid-2000s, when personal training was just becoming mainstream. TLC was airing shows like The Biggest Loser (which we now know to be extremely problematic) and anyone with any means was suddenly interested in working out, one-on-one. I knew how to structure a training session because of the program I'd completed for my degree as well as my background as an athlete, and so the relationship part of personal training came naturally to me. I was genuinely curious about people, and because I knew how much exercise helped me to feel my best, I sincerely wanted to help others find that for themselves, too.

I began getting clients through word of mouth and soon

found that I was training an entire friend group or family because of those referrals. My path was becoming clear. Once I had enough clients, I parted ways with the nurse and opened my own studio. I bought equipment to have a small gym and a home and worked with clients outdoors and at gyms in their buildings.

Because of the cost of personal training, most of my clients were high-earners who referred me to other high-earners. I developed a specialty in working with CEOs who had specific needs based on their schedules, travel plans, and even the ways they sat and moved throughout the day.

It was at the peak of this time in my career that I got a call from a friend about a man she was working with named Garnet. She told me that he was a great client and a kind person, but he rescheduled more than she could accommodate.

Since I didn't mind having to reschedule things, I agreed to take him on.

7. Discomfort: If You're Not Uncomfortable, You're Not Growing

"However it is expressed, the emotional energy underneath hope is 'It's all going to be okay.'"

—Charles Eisenstein

Date: April 18, 2012
Time: 5 a.m.
Session: 81

The waiting room at Stollery Children's Hospital in Edmonton was decorated with colorful tables, chairs, and toys geared towards the hundreds of kids it served each day. I tried to flip through a magazine put on a side table by some considerate soul, but I wouldn't have been able to concentrate on it if it had proof that aliens had landed in my backyard.

Just down the hallway, Keenan was undergoing his pacemaker insertion. At the same time, doctors were determining if he was a candidate for the double switch procedure that would reverse the heart condition he had at birth.

The hospital was the best in all of western Canada. Their surgeons were high-level specialists who did these complex procedures day in and day out. To get there, we'd driven five hours, and I'd had to rearrange my life. I called all my clients and rescheduled them and canceled my Pilates classes for two weeks. I was alone with my thoughts, and it wasn't pleasant.

Just then, a doctor appeared at the door.

"Are you mom?" he said.

"Yes."

"He's done and headed for recovery. He did great. I'd like to give you the results of the surgery, if you're up for it."

I braced myself. "Okay," I said, gripping the sides of my chair. "Yes. Please give them to me."

"I'm sorry to say that he's not a candidate for the double switch. He has a faulty aortic valve, and it would be too risky."

"Will he ever be a candidate? Is it something he could grow into?"

"No. I'm so sorry."

My heart broke into pieces. I'd tried as hard as I could not to get my hopes up about this, but completely stifling my wish that Keenan's condition could be corrected so he could live out his childhood like other kids had proven impossible. I choked back a sob.

"Okay. Thank you. I'm so grateful to you regardless."

She smiled. "Would you like to come sit with him?"

"Yes."

Upon seeing Keenan, I wanted to be brave and convey that all was well and that he shouldn't be concerned. The truth was, it actually wasn't that hard. Whether it was the mind protecting me from future fears or mother bear energy falsely leading me to believe that I could protect Keenan from anything, in that moment, I was simply grateful that, for the foreseeable future, Keenan was still himself: a kind and lovable kid and an unexpected blessing in my life.

———

Two weeks later, we were back in Saskatoon. The surgery had taken a toll on Keenan's body. In children, putting in a pacemaker involves breaking the rib cage, and so Keenan's healing process was slow.

Even so, I was hopeful. I didn't need Keenan to be a professional athlete or even to be as interested in fitness as I was, but it killed me to think he would miss opportunities to play with other kids because he had to sit things out. Small children socialize through physical activity, and I'd already seen him sit out things like pick-up soccer games and playground races.

In the longer term, I was concerned about his health. I knew that many people with heart conditions that prevented physical activity could develop an understandable fear about performing any kind of challenging movement—and that those fears could, in turn, lead to secondary conditions like diabetes or obesity. I desperately hoped that the pacemaker would allow him to start participating in more social activities, meet new friends, and take care of his health into adulthood.

I also didn't know how I would manage my schedule going forward. I was still working up to 10 or 11 hours a day and couldn't afford to cut back, but I needed to be available for Keenan during his recovery. Even working with Garnet, as much as I enjoyed our time together, would be tricky to fit in. As the primary breadwinner, I needed to find a way to make more money, work fewer hours or, ideally, both. It brought me back, face to face, with my idea for pivoting my business—something I'd been avoiding thinking about.

Since I'd made my list of goals, I'd tried pitching my idea to a few existing clients. I thought it would be an easy sell. We already had a good rapport, and the truth that what I wanted to do—be more intentional about incorporating their mental health into our physical workouts—was something we already did together. Inevitably, as I got to know my clients over time, I became a de facto therapist. They would often work out their problems with me during sessions. There's science behind this phenomenon; around 20 minutes into a workout, our defenses begin to go down as our bodies and minds feel better and loosen up. Whether my clients knew it or not, it was what made our sessions special and what made their time with me productive. I rarely pointed it out to them, but once I did, I felt certain they'd be willing to explore it more intentionally with me.

I was wrong. The clients I talked to about it were very enthusiastic about my idea—just not for themselves. One or two even denied talking to me about their problems, as if their minds blacked out how vulnerable they'd allowed themselves to be.

I knew who I needed to talk to.

———

My next session with Garnet was on a blissfully sunny day. The most frigid part of the Saskatchewan winter was beginning to thaw, and I didn't waste any time getting to the point. With our breath visible in the air and the sun sparkling off the snow, I let my frustration pour out. I told Garnet about the barriers I'd run into, how I didn't know what to do next, how I needed to make a drastic change, and that somehow, it would be the path that allowed me to be there for my son.

Ever the empath, Garnet listened patiently.

"So," I said, sniffling, "what do you think I should do?"

Garnet was silent for a moment as my words lingered in the air. I knew I was asking a lot.

I probably sounded ridiculous. I was just about to spiral into a vulnerability hangover when Garnet interrupted my thoughts.

"It never ceases to amaze me what a wonderful mother you are," he said. Not what I was expecting.

"What do you mean?" I asked.

"You rearranged your entire life to get Keenan to that hospital. Now, instead of letting the effort required to care for him drag you into a depression, you're already thinking about how you can change your whole life again."

"Well, of course. What else would I do?"

"I know. It's just not the mother I had."

I was silent. I knew that was true, and it made me so sad for him.

As if he could read my mind, he said, "You don't need to be sad for me. It's just an observation. Now. What should you do next? Well, nothing you haven't already done."

"I'm not sure what you mean."

"When you called your clients to tell them you had to reschedule, I know how hard that was for you. You hate letting people down; it goes against everything you believe in. But you had something more important to take care of, so you let yourself feel that discomfort and you did it anyway. That's what you have to do with your business."

"Call and cancel my existing clients?" The thought made me want to throw up.

"No. Go outside your comfort zone. The goals you made weren't big enough. You cannot achieve the next level of success without experiencing discomfort. That's where growth happens."

This was a new way of thinking about things. I always imagined that getting to a new level with my business would feel good along the way; maybe there would be some bumps, but overall the journey would be gratifying.

I said as much to Garnet, and I thought he stifled a laugh.

"That's not been my experience. Quite the contrary. When I'm pushing myself to accomplish something new, I wake up every day feeling nauseous. That's how much discomfort I experience. It's a constant companion. But the great coach who counseled me from the Buddhist perspective said, when you feel that way, you say to yourself, 'Oh, there's that discomfort again. How wonderful, because this is the discomfort that usually comes before success.' So you recognize it, and you take ownership of it, because if you are not uncomfortable, then you aren't moving outside your little bubble. So you need to take those goals and make them bigger, until you almost can't bear to look at them."

I jogged along silently for a moment. Something inside me was feeling off, as if a long-standing boulder had been pushed aside to reveal a very vulnerable patch of soil. I wanted the boulder back, but I knew that Garnet was right. I hadn't pushed myself hard enough; I'd stayed in my comfort zone, with my existing clients, and then tried to give up after one attempt to change. It reminded me of something I already knew about physical exertion.

"You know, Garnet, there's a great parallel here in sports psychology," I said. "There's a lot of good evidence to show that getting people into a zone of discomfort when they exercise translates to something called 'stress resilience.'"

"I like that name—the Zone of Discomfort," he said. "We have to *choose* to go through it and believe that we will eventually arrive on the other side. First discomfort, then achievement."

"That would mean we have to train our minds to perceive discomfort as something positive instead of as failure or self-doubt," I said.

"Yes. Instead of calling something you did a failure, you say it's not yet a success."

"When you push yourself in this way, where do you feel the discomfort in your body?"

"Well, as I've told you, I often feel nauseous. Sometimes I have racing thoughts or sweaty palms, too."

"I suppose it's also important, though, to know when you're in the Zone of Discomfort because you're being confronted with a limiting belief versus when you're there because your body is actually giving you a warning sign."

"That's true. And I haven't always been great about heeding warning signs."

"If I'm thinking as a parent, I want my kids to know that difference. If something feels dangerous, that's not a situation you push through. The productive discomfort is what you feel when you are nervous about whether or not you'll be successful in an endeavor you believe in."

"Well, as I said, you're a great mom. And the good news is, the practice gets easier with time. You slowly learn how to tolerate the discomfort, and how to remind yourself that it's a necessary step on the journey to growth."

———

The next day, I had about an hour to myself when my partner took my son to the playground. I decided to use it. Without glancing at the list I'd made the week before—which was apparently not specific enough—I grabbed a scrap of paper lying on the kitchen counter and, before my inner critic could make her appearance, scribbled down a list of goals as fast as I could:

<u>GOALS—Three Year Plan</u>
30 speeches per year
Two TED talks
100 new 1-1 clients
100,000 digital subscribers or followers
$250,000 annually

I put my pen down and stared at what I'd written. I wasn't even sure where it came from. Who did I think I was, aiming to make a quarter of a million dollars per year? And why would 100,000 people care what I have to say? To my shock, I began to feel light-headed and my stomach turned. I pictured myself stepping out onto a TED talk stage and...what if there was no one in the audience? What if they laughed me off the stage? What if...I threw up, as I felt I might just looking at the list?

Oh.

This was exactly the feeling Garnet was describing. Audacious—so audacious as to almost make me feel sick. What I really wanted to do was crumple the list up, throw it in the trash, and go about my usual business.

Instead, with my pulse pounding, I ripped it out of my notebook and stuck it to my fridge.

The next morning, Keenan surprised me by coming to the kitchen for breakfast on his own. When he wandered in to hug me, he pointed to the list.

"Mommy, what is this?" he said.

Was I going to make myself accountable to my child? It couldn't hurt.

"Those are my goals for the next three years," I said. "That's what I want to accomplish in order to make things better for our family and for my work."

Keenan looked up at me with his eyes wide. "You can do it, Mommy!" he said. I couldn't help but smile. Maybe my little boy was right.

Things to Think On
Finding Comfort in the Zone of Discomfort

C hange is hard for all of us. Our bodies rebel against it and our minds tell us not to move forward. Even so, we must remember that this discomfort is natural, necessary, and an unavoidable aspect of growth.

We've already discussed writing down our goals, and we should use that practice here as well. Once again, we should make them big, hairy, and audacious. As we do so, we can allow our body to rebel the way it wants to. That's the discomfort, and it should be expected—so how can we work through it? Here are some steps that we can take:

1. Prepare. Through meticulous preparation, we won't have to fly by the seat of our pants, which can compound our anxiety and stop us from taking the action we need to take.

2. Take Constant Action. When we are truly focused on a goal, we shouldn't let a day go by without doing some action that will bring us one step closer to it.

3. Ignore Naysayers. People will doubt our abilities to

reach our goals in implicit and explicit ways, and sometimes these people will be our friends and family. That will be painful, but we must understand that others are doing it from a place of fear or of love. We must remain steadfast.

4. Embrace Mistakes. No one succeeds without mistakes along the way—lots of them. Our goal should not be to avoid mistakes entirely but to learn from them and refine our processes with what we've learned before taking action once again. We should minimize the time we spend in self-pity. Remember: our mistakes are not failures. They are just not complete successes yet.

Being able to fully see, know, and listen to a client is and has been what I enjoy most about my work. The vulnerability, stories, aspirations, and emotions shared during our time together is mutually rewarding, and the birthplace of a life-transforming experience in which the client begins to see themselves as someone strong who can accomplish things physically —and, in turn, mentally—that they didn't think they could.

One of the ways I have understood clients in those sessions was to listen to their stories about their families of origin. Whenever someone asked me if I had a sibling, I said, "I did grow up with a sibling, Cassie, but she died a long time ago." Folks usually didn't know what to say, but despite their discomfort, they almost always followed up by asking how she died.

I've always answered them honestly: "Cassie took her own life." Often, in those moments, people have shrunk back. They're embarrassed for asking the question and worried that their need to know might have caused me pain—our humanness causing us problems again. Even so, I have been fine with it and still am to this day. I feel no stigma around it, and the sadness it brings to talk about it randomly is usually small.

After working together for a while, Garnet and I learned that we shared this kind of tragedy in our backgrounds. I can't remember the particulars, but it was likely prompted by me asking him about his family. For many people who have shared loss, this may have meant momentary empathy or a brief awkwardness in the conversation, but for Garnet and me, it created a kinship. Suddenly, both of us felt the same thing: I know you, I see you, and I hear you.

We recognized a mutual resilience in one another, along with a compassion for others' darkest suffering. A trust came from us exposing the most vulnerable parts of our emotional selves. For both of us, that trust became the birthplace for feeling a sense of true belonging.

Given what we were doing together—running through the freezing cold at 5 a.m. while most sane people were still snug in their beds—we also saw in one another the power to overcome. We were determined to be the people who didn't succumb to the hardships they'd faced. Instead, we wanted to be the catalysts for change.

————

I was pregnant with my second child when I came across the concept of self-compassion in an online behavioral psychology class. Self-compassion is a notion about forgiving yourself for things you felt had not been right in your life and understanding that when you got knocked down, instead of making it worse by beating yourself up, you could find kindness for yourself in those moments. This was something I struggled with mightily, and so, as I did whenever I was excited about a new idea, I went full throttle. I bought books by Kristen Neff, the leading researcher in the field of self-compassion, and studied all I could on the topic.

But six months into my pregnancy, something went wrong. Though I may never know why, I started bleeding and was rushed to the hospital. Within two hours, I had lost the pregnancy.

Being that far along, I'd already bought the baby new clothes and taken time off work. I had already changed the way I would see myself in the world: I was going to be a person with another baby. Now, my heart was shattered, and I plunged into a world of profound grief.

After it happened, I couldn't just go back to work and life and pretend anything was the same. I needed a new trajectory, something—anything—to turn my mind in a different direction. Eventually, I decided to go back to school to get my master's degree.

My first stop was to visit a supervisor who'd taught in my honors program when I was getting my undergraduate degree. I asked him if he would supervise me through graduate studies, and he responded with a yes.

Then he added: "My primary area of research is self-compassion. Have you heard of it?"

In my conversations with Olivia, a story came up that I often like to share whenever I talk about what it takes for people to change: A man is out hiking in the woods, and he hears a dog yelping. He walks towards the sound, and he comes into a clearing. The dog is laying on the deck of a house, and there's an old man in a rocking chair.

The hiker goes up to the old man and says, "Your dog is yelping. I could hear him from all the way over there. He's obviously in pain."

And the old man says, "Yep."

So the hiker says, "Why is he in pain?"

"Because he's lying on a nail," says the old man.

"Why doesn't he move?" says the hiker.

"Well," says the old man, "I guess it doesn't hurt enough yet."

8. Resilience: Fail Hard, Then Get Up off the Mat

"If I never loved, I never would have cried
I am a rock, I am an island..."

— *"I Am a Rock," Simon and Garfunkel*

Date: May 23, 2012
Time: 5 a.m.
Session: 89

My alarm went off at 4 a.m., and as usual, I woke up, got dressed quietly, and went downstairs to make my coffee. But this morning, as with every morning for the past month, I went in to check on Keenan before doing anything else.

He was healing well from his surgery, but it was slow-going. Even so—and even though watching my son go through such an invasive procedure had tested my composure and nervous system more than I ever let on—I was deeply optimistic about what it would mean for his ability to move more freely. Already, he'd been testing the limits of what he could do, even with his bruising and bones still on the mend.

I didn't have time to stop and think about it much, though, because none of what we were going through stopped life from happening. After I adjusted his blankets and left him sleeping soundly in his room, I headed to Garnet's. I had a workout prepared that was going to push him to his maximum output, just as I'd been pushing to my maximum output lately as well.

Since our conversations about the Zone of Discomfort, I'd challenged myself to do everything I possibly could to reach my goals. That meant taking small actions towards them every day, and I had done just that. First, I honed my message to a single line: *I am the best available resource for women seeking to overcome limiting internal and external beliefs through guided workshops that dismantle external messages and foster self-discovery.*

Then, I reached out to all my existing clients and asked for referrals. And I began writing talks that I could give to small groups to build my way up to larger presentations on larger stages.

But instead of taking me on my way to the next level of success, I wasn't getting any takers. My new approach to pitching clients involved talking openly about something that often happens in personal training sessions organically: clients use me as a therapist. I mean that in the best way; I love talking to people and helping them remove barriers as well as addressing the psychological problems that inevitably get in the way of personal growth. My hope was that we could deliberately incorporate that element of our work—the unspoken element—into our time together. I saw this as potentially revolutionizing fitness by openly acknowledging that it is a mind-body connection, and that physical health and mental health do not exist on separate planes.

But when I lobbed the idea to my clients, most said they'd rather keep their mental health and physical health separate, despite the fact that they were already, and inextricably, intertwined.

My mind was blown by this discovery. I suddenly had the realization that I'd been thinking about this idea so often and for so much longer than most people had that what I was suggesting to them was barely making sense, let alone selling them on a new way of working together. As I talked to one client after another to confirm this, I figured out in real time that they were not as far down this particular continuum as I had been.

Hearing all that feedback had two effects on me. One was that I wondered if I'd been kidding myself about having something new and valuable to offer at all. The other was that I realized that if I did continue believing in what I wanted to offer clients—and I did—I needed to either get better at educating them or get clearer with my messaging.

I was so deep into this thinking that I planned to launch right into it as soon as Garnet and I found our running groove. But when I saw him at the door, I could tell something was off. He was chilly and only answered my attempts at conversation with monosyllables.

"Garnet," I finally said, after 15 minutes of jogging in silence, "is something on your mind?"

"I lost a major client over the weekend, and it was no one's fault but my own," he said.

I found myself stunned. I'd spent so much time talking with him about my business that I forgot he had his own to attend to. And since he was already so successful, I realized at that

moment that I'd assumed he never made mistakes anymore—
not big ones, anyway.

"I'm so sorry," I said. "That really...sucks." I wished I could
come up with something more eloquent, but it was the best I
could do.

To my surprise, Garnet let out a chuckle. "It does suck," he
said. "You're right."

"Do you want to talk about it?"

"Not in detail, but I'll tell you that it was a huge client who
would have made millions for the company."

"How did you lose them?"

"I played hardball and lost. I'm normally very collaborative
when I meet a prospective client, but I was overconfident and
unyielding in negotiations this time, and it didn't work."

"Oh, man. That must feel awful."

"It does. But it's not the first time it's happened, and it
won't be the last."

"What are you going to do?"

"I'm going to get back up off the mat and keep trying."

I had to laugh. "Garnet, I think I just answered my own
question."

"Oh? How so?"

"I was going to tell you that I've begun to feel like a failure.
I've been trying to pitch my new business to my existing clients
and no one's taking me up on it, and I don't know what to do
next."

"Ah. Well, then yes, I think you did. Failure is part of the
process of trying. If you haven't failed, you probably haven't
tried your hardest. And you should always be aiming to do your
best, not your fifth best. But, I'll ask you, because you're the pro
—what do *you* suggest *I* do to help myself get back out there?"

I wasn't used to being on the receiving end of this line of
questioning, but a thought immediately popped into my mind.

"Well, this reminds me a lot of my work in self-compassion, and what we tell people to do is to turn inward and speak kindly to themselves in these moments. The research has found that the most common thing people say to themselves, and what actually makes them feel better, is, 'I'm okay, I've got this, I'm just fine.' It's so simple, but it's so universally soothing."

"I'm going to challenge you on that, Olivia, because for me to say 'I'm just fine,' that may be true, but I've let my team down. I need to say, 'I'm just fine,' and then I need to examine what made me do what I did, understand it, and take responsibility with my employees and partners. Why did this really fail? What am I not prepared to look at about myself, about the situation? I have to face the reality of it. This goes back to what we talked about months ago, about doing what you say you'll do and living in alignment with your core values."

"Well, yes, but you want to be sure to give yourself a moment of really feeling that sense of 'I'm okay.' Otherwise you're just beating yourself up. The Buddha calls it the second arrow. You were hit with an arrow when you failed, but if you're then really hard on yourself, it's like shooting yourself with another arrow that's as painful as the first arrow."

"So, how do you avoid doing that?"

"We want to fully accept the pain of the first arrow, speak kindly to ourselves, and then take the steps needed to move forward."

"I can reframe that. It's about understanding what's undone or what remains to be done. So, what is it that I can still do? That's what I think about all the time. In your case, it seems like it has to do with continuing the work of educating your clients."

"So what motivates you to get up off the mat?"

"Well, one thing I do is that I remind myself that there's so much more to be done. There are so many more people I could help. And if I quit at this moment, I'd be letting all those people down."

"What else?"

"I let myself feel the pain. Meaning, when I have a problem, when I've done something wrong or made a mistake—which happens to everybody, by the way—I hurt. I don't fake it, I don't push it away or numb it with drugs, alcohol, shopping, food, whatever. I let myself feel the pain of that first arrow."

"Right, yes. Because if you don't let yourself feel the pain, you can almost excuse yourself from attending to the problem. Then time will pass and you'll never have dealt with it. In order to have the energy to deal with it, you have to really let yourself experience how awful it is. And that's not easy."

"No, it's not. And if you really want to challenge yourself, you can decide not to feel sorry for yourself throughout this process."

"That's a tall order!"

"Well, but feeling sorry for yourself makes it too easy to give yourself an excuse not to try again. Think about what you and I have both overcome already, Olivia. Family suicides. Sexual abuse. We got up off the mat from those experiences. That was not easy, but we did it. If we can do it for that, we can do it for anything. You have to remember what you've already overcome."

I was quiet for a moment as I let that sink in, and I found my mind going back to Keenan. Here was this small child, already overcoming so much. I wanted him to look back on this time, even if he didn't remember it perfectly, and know how strong he was, what he was capable of surviving—and how he went on to thrive. In order for him to be able to do that, I had to model it.

"In self-compassion work, this has a lot to do with believing that you are completely worthy and capable and lovable, including the parts of you that you perceive as flaws and imperfections," I said. "If I believe that is true, then I can expose myself to a flaw about myself, because it doesn't change my worth and value."

"Failure is not personal," said Garnet. "It's a part of growth."

Things to Think On
Failing Hard and Getting off the Mat Again

There is no success without failure. As a result, the earlier we embrace failure as part of our process, the sooner we will be equipped to move forward in a courageous and informed way. Though we will inevitably hit bumps in the road and feel discouraged, we don't have to remain there. Whenever that happens, there are still steps we can take to get back on track:

1. Acknowledge Our Feelings: After recognizing that we didn't get where we wanted to be or we didn't reach a certain goal, we should sit with that disappointment for a moment—but while remembering how far you've come.

2. Self-Soothe: Once our disappointment has eased, we should remind ourselves that we're going to be okay—*because we are.*

3. Identify Any Errors: Were we being true to our values? Did we do our best? Was there anything we could have done differently, now that we have the benefit of hindsight? In particular, were we humble?

4. Identify Next Steps: What positive actions can we take? These might include a different approach, getting a coach or teacher or simply calling someone who had a similar experience and asking for their advice.

It was a beautiful morning, and Garnet and I were enjoying the peacefulness on the trail. I was explaining to him this feeling that I got with clients, where they often share so much about themselves and let me into their personal lives that it seems to me as though we've become friends.

"But the thing that always happens," I said as we jogged along, "is that I'll get them something for an anniversary or big occasion, I'll get their kid something for their birthday, and sometimes I feel foolish for having thought the relationship was perhaps a bit deeper than it really was."

Without missing a beat, Garnet replied, "Well, you're their employee."

His words hit me like a punch to the gut. By this point, we'd been working together for over half a year. He took Keenan out on adventures and provided me with profound life advice. To hear myself described that way by him, of all people, was so painful that I stopped dead in my tracks.

"What?" he said.

I tried to stay neutral, but to my shock and embarrassment, the words came out with tears.

"I just can't believe you said that," I said. "It's not that I don't know they've hired me, but that's just so...cold."

I sniffled and wiped my eyes for long enough to see the color drain out of his face. He's rarely at a loss for words, but he was in that moment.

"I didn't mean that they don't like you," he said. "I just meant...oh, I feel awful. I'm so sorry."

"You could have found a kinder way to say that."

"I could have. Of course. What can I do?"

"No, nothing. I'm okay."

"You're not okay. I do have eyes."

I laughed. Leave it to Garnet to make me smile in a moment like this. "It's just that I really put my whole self into my work *and my relationships with clients, and to hear that I'm just someone they pay and nothing more, it's a very painful way to think about it."*

"I know. I don't think of you that way. To me, you are a friend. And a good one."

I'd never heard him articulate that before, and I knew he was not a person who would say something like that just to make me feel better. He was making himself quite vulnerable, and I was suddenly overwhelmed with the urge to give him a hug.

This wasn't a new feeling for me—I'm a hugger and usually embrace my friends readily—but Garnet holds himself in a way that indicates he needs personal space. He's always warm, but never physically affectionate in the slightest.

But in that moment, I realized that our friendship had become close enough for me to override his discomfort. I'd assumed that I was as important to him as he was to me, but him saying it aloud validated the friendship. I flung my arms out wide, and wrapped them around him.

It turned out to be a memorable moment because at six-foot-two, Garnet is nearly a foot taller than me. When I hugged him, I felt like a little girl, hugging his tummy. And because of his discomfort with physical affection, he wasn't quite sure how to respond. He remained stiff but returned the embrace.

It was one of the most awkward hugs of my life, but it was also one of the most important. That was when I knew we were really friends.

9. Our Uniqueness Means Our Idiosyncrasies Are Superpowers

"And the day came when the risk to remain tight in a bud was more painful than the risk it took to blossom."

—*Anaïs Nin*

Date: June 7, 2012
Time: 5 a.m.
Session: 92

We were one month away from Kananaskis, and our energy around the event was driving our workout sessions. Garnet and I had spent months recruiting and organizing a team of ten runners—the race required that each participant take a 10-mile leg of the relay—and decided that I would take Leg 5, which is largely uphill, and Garnet would take Leg 9. The rest of our group was made up of members of Garnet's Saturday running group, as well as a few people to whom we'd been connected through friends.

Garnet's leg would take him through a sloping valley with a stunning view of the mountains, and I wanted to make sure he could do it with no complications. In part, I wanted him to enjoy the experience; he'd worked so hard during our training sessions and had come so far since we began working together. Additionally, I wanted to ensure he didn't run into any physical difficulties. His calf muscle hadn't loosened up much, and the last thing he needed was to be stalled by a bad cramp. To combat that possibility as best we could, I gave him tips to minimize problems that might arise from all the airline travel and prolonged sitting he was doing for work. In the week leading up to this session, I'd tasked Garnet with running every day. As we jogged along our usual trail, I could tell he'd been doing it.

"Garnet, the difference in your endurance is amazing," I said. "Not just this week, but thinking back to where you were physically in our first few months of sessions."

"Well, that's all thanks to you," he said. "Remember what I told you? When I decided to make this big change in my life, it was because of that run through Toronto Airport that left me huffing and puffing and dripping with sweat."

"I'll never forget it."

We ran in silence for a few minutes. The sun rises very early in Saskatoon in the spring, so unlike our dark winter runs, we were bathed in sunlight and warmth. The light reflected off the Saskatchewan River in tiny diamonds, giving the morning a bit of a magical quality. Garnet broke the silence with something he'd been keeping close tabs on.

"How is Keenan doing?" he said.

"He's great," I said, and it was true. It had been two months since his surgery and while he was still not at 100 percent, he was up and running around. The most amazing thing to me was his fearlessness; he was anxious to move his body in ways he couldn't before. This was all I could have asked from the procedure—to discover that he wasn't fearful of movement based on the constraints he'd been under prior to the pacemaker. It was a relief, and it was a joy to see my boy full of energy and uninhibited.

"I'm so glad," said Garnet.

"I know," I said. "And actually, I wanted to ask you something, too."

"Go ahead."

"Could you tell me more about your ADHD diagnosis? We're starting to think that Keenan might have it too, based on some feedback we've gotten from his teachers."

"Of course. And to be honest with you, Olivia, I have thought the same thing about Keenan. It's strange to see so many similarities between Keenan and myself at that age."

"So how have you managed your diagnosis?"

"Well, you have to remember that I didn't get mine until I was forty years old. But the main thing is, people with ADHD are big risk-takers—beyond what might be considered normal—and we can be very impulsive. For me, that looked like making high-risk financial decisions on a whim that ultimately led to bankruptcy.

"I was on the path to changing my behavior when I got that diagnosis, and it helped me to have a framework for some of my actions that I didn't understand. I began to read books and use assessment tools like Kolbe, Strengthsfinder, and Myers-Briggs. Studying Buddhism also helped me understand the nature of my mind and consciousness."

"That sounds like a lot of work."

"It was. But the silver lining of how my ADHD expresses itself is that I have an incredible amount of mental energy. So I didn't spend much time feeling sorry for myself. I went into problem-solving mode. Now, I'm more measured and patient, and much more collaborative."

"That's so interesting. So your ADHD has almost become your superpower."

"Not almost—it *has* become my superpower. We all have them—characteristics and personality traits that make us unique that can either be our downfall or our personal pathway to success. You just have to make sure they're working for you instead of against you."

I knew immediately, without even thinking about it, what some of those traits were in me.

I was an overthinker. I loved to get into the weeds when I was passionate about something, but sometimes I got stuck there. I had big goals for spreading my ideas and messages, but wasn't confident that anyone wanted to hear them.

Garnet, as usual, could tell what I was thinking.

"One of your many superpowers, Olivia, is your intelligence and perfectionism. You don't want to do something unless it's unassailable. This makes your work excellent, but it also means you don't put nearly as much of that work out into the world as you could."

"Guilty as charged!"

"So how could you embrace your Olivia-ness and challenge yourself to take bigger risks?"

"How about if I borrow some of your extreme risk-taking sensibility, and you borrow some of my reluctance to take risks?"

"I don't need it anymore. You should see my daily routines and rules. I come home and my keys go in one spot. I delegate my time to the minute. I also take medication to help me manage. Sorry, you have to find it on your own!"

Sometimes I thought Garnet got deep joy out of putting me on the spot.

"Fine," I said. "Well, in *addition* to what I'm doing to push myself, I was thinking about starting a podcast. And if I'm being honest, what's holding me back is the idea of recording something and then just...releasing it out into the world."

"That's a wonderful idea, and it would be a great challenge. What would the podcast be about?"

"I'm not totally sure yet. Maybe interviews with other experts in the field of health and fitness who see the culture in the same way I do."

"What would it take for you to start that?"

"A stiff drink?"

"Ha, ha. I can't wait to hear the first episode."

Things to Think On
Finding, Embracing and Implementing Our You-ness

We all have qualities and characteristics that could bolster our success or bring us down. The key is to find those qualities, get honest with ourselves about how we currently wield them, and make changes as necessary.

There are many personality tests we can take as a starting point. After completing one of them, we can use that context to think about how various characteristics play out in our lives. Some questions we can ask are:

- How do I currently use these personal characteristics?
- In what ways do they hold me back?
- How could I harness them in a way that feels doable but challenging to help me reach my goals?

From there, we can use the tools from Chapter 2 to plan out the steps to take towards implementing any changes.

My visualization coach had tasked me with what seemed like a straightforward exercise: "Sit on this couch," he said, "and visualize where you want to be in three years."

I closed my eyes and began breathing. We normally did guided visualizations together, but for this, I let my mind wander wherever it wanted to go. As I let my thoughts melt away, what I didn't realize was that I was about to have a two-part visualization that would change my perspective on my life.

My dad and I had long been estranged, but there had been periodic visits over the years. He had met Keenan a few times and called here or there out of the blue. Gradually, however, he had fallen completely out of touch. And walking into my visualization, I realized I hadn't talked to him in over a decade. It had come to a point where I had no real way to track him down and no real idea whether he was alive or dead.

I was struggling with the realization that I hadn't forgiven him for not wanting to be part of my life. I wanted to be in his life, but he didn't want to be in mine. It made me so sad. I was trying to come to a place of peace about it, because it felt like it was holding me back emotionally in some way.

As I let my body relax into the couch and allowed my mind to wander, my dad came to me—and all of a sudden, I felt so much warmth and love towards him and from him. I realized that the reason I felt so sad about our relationship was because I loved him so much. It was such a gift to feel so much love, because deep down and despite everything, I knew he did love me and that I loved him. Even though I didn't get to have him in my life, I still had that gift of knowing I was loved.

After that, the visualization transitioned, and I saw my father as he was when my sister and I were children. He was really fun, and I remembered that that had been one of the things I loved most about him. Sometimes, he would sit down on the floor and play with us—or when we were driving in the car, he would tell us stories of Jason and the Argonauts and other tales from Greek mythology, some of them real myths and some just things that he made up. He would tell those stories to my sister and me as well as our four cousins. As he did, we would invent what happened next, and he would build on it, with us hanging on his every word. As I saw all these things in my visualization, the phrases that came to mind to describe it were "gift of gab" and "charismatic."

"I gave them to you," I heard him say to me. "You love them about me, but they're also in you." It was an overwhelming feeling: I had somehow made a contract with my dad. That contract said that he wouldn't be in my life, but he would remain in me. He'd given me these gifts, and even if they were the only ones remaining, I still had to use them. They were Spirit-given gifts that I needed to work out, and my life would never be fulfilled until I did.

Through that experience, I no longer questioned whether or not he loved me. Instead, I began choosing to have gratitude for what my father had already given me rather than grieving what I was missing. In his own way, he'd taught me what it meant to feel deep love for another person. As strange as it sounded, with all things considered, I was so appreciative he had chosen to be my dad despite the losses I'd endured. For now, that was enough for me.

We'd been running along in silence for about 10 minutes, enjoying the fresh air and quiet before we started our hectic days. All of a sudden, Garnet broke in.

"This trail is so beautiful," he said. "It reminds me of something I used to do with my kids."

"Oh yeah?" I said. "What's that?"

"We traveled a lot, even when we couldn't afford it, so they could see the beauty and diversity in different parts of the world," he said. "They saw the ruins at Chichén Itzá. They couldn't stop talking about it for days."

"That's a wonderful memory," I said.

"I wanted them to be able to notice the magic in life," he said, "no matter what else was going on."

10. Chosen Family

"I get by with a little help from my friends..."

—*"With a Little Help from My Friends,"* Joe Cocker

Date: July 12, 2012
Time: 5 a.m.
Session: 100

The Kananaskis 100 Mile Relay was first held in 1987, and it has since become a beloved race among seasoned relay runners and newcomers alike. Known for its magnificent scenery and challenging elevation, it's one of the most difficult but rewarding competitions in Canada.

By the time we landed in Alberta, Garnet and I were ready. He was easily able to complete a 10-mile run, and I'd been pushing myself by training on terrain that mirrored the literal uphill battle I'd have on my leg of the run.

The morning of the race, a stunning sunrise painted the sky

in reds and oranges. We watched in awe as we made our way to the starting line. By the time the first runners took off, rain had begun to fall and would continue to do so throughout the day. We were in for a wet run.

The first leg of the race began in the foothills of Longview, Alberta. Our lead-off runner covered a stretch of Highway 541, which travels up to the Canadian Rockies. From there, the course was increasingly hilly, until it hit a peak elevation of 2,206 meters above sea level on Highwood Pass, the highest paved mountain pass in the country.

My leg was the fifth, the one that reached the peak elevation and was notoriously the most difficult. When my turn came, I went as hard as I could. Starting off at a brisk pace, I couldn't help but think back to the year Garnet and I had spent training together. We'd come so far—not just physically, although he had made incredible strides in his health, but emotionally and relationally. Although he rarely talked about it, Garnet was in a dark place when we met. He took his divorce hard and blamed himself for everything that went wrong in his marriage. Now, I watched him find real joy in his weekend runs, the time he spent with Keenan, and the time we spent talking during our workout sessions.

For me, I was still reeling from how much he'd shared with me, advice he wished he'd known when he was my age. I trained a lot of CEOs, and it was rare for them to ask about my personal life, let alone try to help me with it. Because of the wisdom Garnet passed on, I felt I had a better trajectory for my next steps. I knew it would be hard work, but I also knew I had a friend in my corner.

I reached the peak of the Highland Pass and took a moment to look around. The view was stunning, as promised. I could see charcoal-colored mountains, crystalline lakes, and hills upon hills of spruce trees splayed out beneath me. It was awe-inspiring, and it occurred to me that I couldn't have done it without the runners in my group who came before me. Without their effort and all of our teamwork, none of this journey would have been possible.

———

Our last runner crossed the finish line just as the sun was setting. We all met up in Kananaskis Village, a remote but beautiful community full of outdoor recreation, and the runners and support teams celebrated with a post-race meal and party at the Pomeroy Kananaskis Mountain Lodge.

I quickly found Garnet and the rest of our team. "We did it!" I said, giving high fives all around.

"We did!" said Garnet, giving me an unexpected hug. "I knew we could."

Our team was thrilled with our outcome. We didn't come in first, but that was never the point. Garnet met one of his fitness goals—being able to run 10 miles—and we both created a wonderful community of supportive friends who also strove to be the best version of themselves.

Later, as we ate plates full of barbecue around a firepit, Garnet and I talked more about that community. He'd shared with me months ago that he was plagued with regret for all the time he spent working instead of being with his ex-wife and children. While he felt it was necessary financially at the time, he also saw some of his workaholic tendencies passed on to his daughters. As he grew older and did more self-reflection, he saw that what mattered most was love and relationships. Now, he said, that idea was evolving into the notion of a chosen family.

"I didn't have much of a family, and I've lost many people

over the years," he said. "So now, I'm starting to realize that I can choose who I want to be a part of my family."

"Do you ever worry about making yourself vulnerable?" I asked. "That people will take advantage of you?"

"I start off every relationship on the basis of trust, and people have to earn their way out," he said. "I still believe in the goodness of our fellow man every day, all the time, and I also know that, yes, there are people out there who will take advantage of kindness. It's still heartbreaking at times, and it's always disappointing. Not everybody deserves to be in your circle. But you can't let yourself become completely closed off out of fear."

"I've had people in my life like that, Garnet, and what I find is that I end up feeling resentment towards them if they try to take advantage of me. And that's something I want to avoid."

"I've been thinking about this a lot lately, Olivia, because I don't have anyone in my biological family who I can trust or turn to. So I'll tell you how family has been framed for me. I have people I'm close to, and a lot of different people in my life that I help. But I recently had a meeting with Rich Christiansen, who is a very successful entrepreneur, and he started to dedicate his life to helping wealthy families go through succession. When we were meeting with him, I brought up the fact that I had people around me that..."

Garnet paused, and I could see that he was choking back tears.

"People that I wished were my kids," he said. "So, Rich went through an analogy of what constituted family, and he said, 'Family is someone who would take a bullet for you.' That brought me up short. I never had people like that in my biological family. But right off the bat, as soon as he said that, I could think of at least one person in my life who met that description.

"*That*," he added, "is chosen family."

Before I knew it, I was wiping away tears as well. I'd also never had that relationship with my biological family, and I knew it would be something I would grapple with for the rest of my life, even as I continued my healing journey. Still, hearing Garnet say it reframed for me: there was nothing wrong with me because I didn't fit into the family I was born into, but none of us could do life all on our own. It may have been more challenging to find a chosen family, but the way Garnet said it made me know it was worth it.

Things to Think On
We Are Who We Surround Ourselves With

Whether or not we have a strong relationship with our family of origin, we always have the choice of who we let into our lives as we get older.

Family is comprised of the people we love, who will be there for us and vice versa no matter what. We can keep ourselves open to those people and to the idea that our family can always be growing, changing, and expanding—by opening our hearts, learning to trust, and choosing to be vulnerable.

At the same time, we must practice making the difficult choice of letting someone go if they are taking advantage of us or not returning our kindness. It will hurt, but in the end, we will find ourselves surrounded by people we can count on—and who can count on us.

Everything described in this book points to being trustworthy and doing what's right. If we want people we can count on, they need to be able to count on us, too. That's what family is—and it's what all of our families could be, no matter how we got them.

As we meet new people, we should keep in mind that some will be acquaintances, some will be friends, and a select few may turn out to be our family. To help us figure out how close we should decide to become with a person, these are some helpful questions we can ask ourselves:

- How do I feel after seeing this person? You should feel better about yourself, uplifted, not brought down, insulted, or discouraged.
- What are this person's values, and how do they align with mine?
- Is this person striving for continual growth, and do they encourage me to do the same?

Not everyone needs to become our chosen family; in fact, very few people should. By using these questions, we can determine how much to let someone in and when it would be better to let them go.

After my siblings died, it took eight years before I was able to begin processing their deaths. In August, I told my wife that I wanted a divorce. Our marriage wasn't working and hadn't been for years, but in my heart, I still felt profound guilt. I suspected that I could have done more to save the relationship if I'd had the tools. More than that, though, I left when things were going well in my life. My wife had stuck it out with me through all my years of rowdy living and through a bankruptcy—and now, the moment I was on a good track again, I was deciding to leave.

That fall had gone fine, but during the holidays, things were different. As they approached, I noticed that my loneliness and guilt were getting worse. On Christmas Day, I spent the day with my daughter, though my ex-wife was there as well. Knowing I wasn't welcome to stay overnight, I left and drove to my youngest sister's house, but my sister had her own problems. She was struggling with addiction, and so the visit was a disaster; I left soon after I arrived. As I drove away, the night was getting darker and the roads less visible, and I started to unravel. On my way home, I got two speeding tickets 25 minutes apart—and when I walked through my door, I fell to pieces, overwhelmed by my own thoughts. I was so scared that I called a friend of mine, who was a doctor.

I wasn't sure if I was really all that close to the edge, but the thoughts were there. I was thinking about my family and how some of them had already died young. I was starting to wonder if I had the same mental makeup.

"I don't know what to do," I told my friend. "I don't want to do what my mind is telling me to, but all the thoughts are there." My friend talked me through it and got me back to a stable state of mind, but the experience shook me to my core.

I returned to counseling in the winter and spring, and my therapist insisted that it was necessary for me to confront my pain and trauma, to loosen the tightly held knots in my emotional core. Most important to address were two episodes that still haunted me: the feeling of being left to die in the car as a child and the suicides of my two siblings.

My therapist suggested a retreat called Come Alive. Run by an organization called The Haven, the retreat took place on Gabriola Island in British Columbia. Situated on the water's edge, participants stayed for one or several weeks in rustic cabins surrounded by lush woods. After doing some research, I saw the facility helped people work through trauma in group therapy and exercise as well as Chinese acupuncture.

I agreed to attend and arrived on a Sunday, when the weather was beautiful. It was fall, the leaves were changing color and there was a cool breeze coming off the water. I spent that day settling in and getting to know my cohort and the campus. The next day, I began my acupuncture treatment, and that was when things broke open. I was visualizing the moment my mother closed the door behind me on field day, certain I was going to die alone on the floor of the car. Soon, I began to sob— and as I wept, I started to struggle to breathe.

I was having an asthma attack, and I hadn't had one since I was 16.

Several of the coaches at The Haven took me to a private room and sat with me as I released all my repressed pain and fear. In all, we were in that room for four hours. But I still wasn't done.

A few days later, I did another acupuncture session, this time focusing on the deaths of my siblings. As the grief began to wash over me, I recognized something I hadn't identified until then: guilt. Part of me had been clinging to the idea that I could have saved them, that their deaths were somehow my fault. If I'd been closer to my sister or had paid my brother's bills, I thought, *maybe things could've been different. I began to release the idea that the deaths were my fault, and once again, I was sobbing. With that release came the belief that I might let them go, let them rest in peace—and allow myself to find some peace, too.*

Epilogue

"In the end, only kindness matters."

—Jewel

After Garnet and I flew back from Kananaskis, our training sessions became less frequent, but we didn't lose touch—quite the opposite. Our friendship continued to deepen, and I often went to him with personal and business concerns. Since my own father was out of my life, I was deeply grateful for someone in his position to offer advice, but my relationship with Garnet was taken to the next level when, after much soul-searching, I ended my relationship with Keenan's dad. Garnet owned a condo in Saskatoon, and he insisted on renting it to me at a price I could afford.

Without that offer, I would not have been able to make that change in my life. I would have been stuck in a relationship that, while loving, was not working for myriad other reasons. But as someone who struggled deeply with trust, the offer also proved that Garnet was really going to be there for me. He didn't *need* to rent the condo to me; he could have leased it to someone else for more money. He did it because he truly wanted me and Keenan to be okay.

As our friendship evolved, we also never stopped challenging one another. After Garnet remarried, he and his wife committed to the idea of chosen family. They both had children from previous marriages but no real connection to their families of origin, and they shared a vision of welcoming people who feel like family into their closest inner circle. They both felt strongly that family was the most important thing in life.

After about five years, our families were very close. I'd remarried as well and had settled into a new place in Saskatoon. One day, Garnet told me he'd invited Keenan into his chosen family. I was floored and very hurt. Years ago, I would have kept that to myself, soldiered on, and pretended to be happy for Keenan while nursing a deep wound. I would not have had the courage to speak up. But Garnet and I had built the kind of friendship where I felt safe in telling him how I really felt.

"That's incredibly generous," I said, "but what about me?"

Garnet later told me that hearing me say that was like a dagger in his heart. He'd been looking at it from the perspective that I was married, had a stable family life, and that he was trying to expand Keenan's support system.

"I just felt horrid," he said. "I hadn't thought about it that way, but as soon as you said that, I thought, *How could I not have seen it this way?*"

Garnet expanded his invitation to include me as well. It's nontraditional, and we understand that. But it's the version of family that makes sense to our little unit. Plus, Garnet's ability to hear me in that moment had a profound effect, because it helped chip away at one of my most stubborn bricks: the one that doesn't allow me to trust myself.

Taking risks like standing up for yourself might mean facing rejection or getting hurt in some other way. But sometimes, it helps you find your way up.

The year that Garnet and I spent training together, teaching one another, and learning and growing together, remains one of the most pivotal years of my life. It was, all told, hundreds of runs—and stretches, and weightlifting—as well as so many life-changing lessons I'll never forget.

Conclusion: Living Life with Integrity

"The problem with the world is that we draw the circle of our family too small."

—Mother Teresa

In the end, what matters most in life is that we live with integrity. Without integrity—which Webster's dictionary defines as "the quality of being honest and having strong moral principles; moral uprightness"—a successful life, one where we can look ourselves in the mirror every day and know we are living up to the person we were put on this earth to be, is not possible.

Each of the chapters in this book outlines one aspect of the work that goes into developing the principles and behaviors we need to live in alignment with the best versions of ourselves. To summarize those points, below are some ideas to help develop each facet of our own integrity:

Bricks

Identifying the belief system that was instilled in us at a young age can be one of the most challenging parts of this process. We should remember to ask ourselves: have we been honest about what our bricks are? Have we excavated our family belief system and identified the false limitations that others have imposed on us and our capabilities?

Habits

After identifying our bricks, it's time to get to the hard work of removing them. When we begin to plot out the habits we want to change, we need to be sure we aren't making excuses for ourselves. Are we justifying our bad habits or reinforcing an old belief system that tells us we're unable to change them?

Dreams

Dreams are what we truly want, what our hearts desire. When we picture our dreams, are they coming from our own imagination or from someone else's ideas for our lives? Are they what we truly want for ourselves?

Values

Of all the facets of integrity and moving past outdated belief systems, identifying our values and living by them is among the most important. Here, we have to ask ourselves if we have invested enough time into self-reflection to accurately pinpoint what's most important to us. And after we've done that, are we ready to accept that living by our values is a lifelong journey? One that requires being honest with ourselves every single day?

Generosity

Often when we think of generosity, we think of it in terms of giving—perhaps financially, or perhaps of our time. But generosity involves much more than that. It means doing what we say we'll do, when we say we'll do it. It also means doing the right thing—the thing that reflects our values, even when that thing is very unpleasant. That is the true spirit of giving.

Goals

Too often, we talk about what we want to do, have or be without making any concrete plans to achieve or attain whatever we're aiming for. This not only doesn't move us forward, but it reinforces the notion that we can't have or do what we want. Making *specific* goals is a foundational element of achieving our dreams. When we find that we're doing more talking than action-taking, it's time for us to put pen to paper and create a plan for ourselves.

Discomfort

The truth about setting goals is that the road to achieve them is going to be bumpy. If we're doing it right, it's going to take us far outside of our comfort zone. But here's the good news: being uncomfortable is how we know we're doing it right. By discovering ways to move through that discomfort, such as using deep breathing or mantras, we will get to the next phase of our life with integrity.

Resilience

When we hit those inevitable setbacks on the road to our goals, we must return to a place of honesty. What went wrong and why? We can't always control obstacles—in fact, they are usually out of our control—but we can control how we respond to them. We can examine our setbacks and see if there was anything we could have done differently. Again, we must *be honest*—and then, we must get back up off the mat.

Unique You

As we make our way down the path to success, we can begin to recognize those things about ourselves that make us unique. These could be strengths or weaknesses; the point is that those chips in your armor, those dings on the surface are what make us special. They are what make us who we are, what make us able to execute and live our own lives in the way that's best for us—not our family of origin, not our boss, not our friends. We are our own secret weapon and our own guiding light.

Chosen Family

Who is in our inner circle? We've all heard the old saying, "You are who you surround yourself with." Are we choosing to spend time with people who uplift us, people who would take a bullet for us—and are we doing the same for them?

Appendix I
Questions to Ask Yourself
Throughout Life

When we begin to get honest with ourselves, we learn that nothing can be accomplished in life without looking in the mirror and being brutally truthful. This is one of the hardest things anyone can do, and it takes years and years of practice.

That's partly because we all have different versions of ourselves, different hats that we wear at varying times which can make us wonder who our true self is. When we return to our childhood homes after having lived by ourselves, for instance, we may naturally regress back to wanting someone else to do our laundry and clean the dishes. It's not because we're incompetent or irresponsible; rather, it's because who we are can change based on the people we're with and the context we find ourselves in.

And yet, underneath the layers of social norms, wrong and right, perfectionism and rebellion, there are versions of each of us that are closer to who we truly believe we are.

As we answer these questions, we need to consider both our past and our future. Who are we now, and who do we want to become? We can't offer answers based on "should"—what we think we *should* do or who we think we *should* be. We must make the choices for which our heart yearns.

The answers to these questions will change and evolve, as we all will throughout the course of our lives. That means we need to be curious about ourselves from now until our last day on Earth.

We must always remember that small things add up. This book is designed to inspire the imagination. It asks us to consider what may once have seemed impossible—though that doesn't mean that only major actions will change our future. Most change happens in tiny baby steps, sometimes even with just an intention. Consistently making our bed in the morning matters as much as getting good grades. Sending a thank-you card puts as much love into the world as a charitable donation. Small things don't matter because of the change they make in the world; they matter because of how they add up and because of the changes they make in us.

To get started on this beautiful journey of ongoing self-knowledge, below are some questions we can ask ourselves whenever we feel stuck:

When We Want to Break a Habit:

1. To what problem is this a solution?
2. Are the choices I made today in alignment with who I want to be and what is important to me?
3. With what can I replace this habit?

When We're Met with a Life Challenge:

1. How have I conquered this type of challenge in the past?

2. If I haven't faced something similar, how have I conquered *other* challenges in the past?
3. Who can I ask for help?

When We're Feeling Lost or Stuck:

1. Am I living by my values?
2. What are the limiting actions or beliefs that have led me to this place?
3. Is fear holding me back?

When We're Faced with a Hard Decision:

1. What is my heart telling me?
2. Which choice is in alignment with my values?
3. Is there a limiting belief telling me I can't do or have one of these choices?

When We're Experiencing Success:

1. What were the behaviors and actions that got me here?
2. Who is this success helping, besides me?
3. What's next?

A Visualization Exercise for When We're Feeling Stuck:

Imagine that you are in your senior years. You're sitting in a lovely garden, contemplating the life you've lived. Looking back at the time between then and now, you feel a deep sense of satisfaction, joy, and contentment. Even though there have been challenges and life was sometimes unkind, you have managed to remain true to yourself to the best of your ability.

What qualities and personal values are represented in that life? Notice any activities that let you know you're living in accord with these values.

Appendix II
Reading List

A critical element of being coachable is reading. Hundreds of great books are available to help us along on our journey, but these are some of our favorites. We compiled this list by thinking about the books that have made the biggest difference in our lives.

Tuesdays with Morrie by Mitch Albom

When a beloved professor is diagnosed with a terminal illness, a former student realizes he only has a limited amount of time to revisit their conversations together. In the process, the student—now a grown man—learns to understand what really matters in life.

Radical Compassion by Tara Brach

Mindfulness teacher Tara Brach offers a meditation practice known as RAIN (Recognize, Allow, Investigate, Nurture). Brach's goal is to coax readers into moving through limiting beliefs and painful feelings, and to find space to move forward in wisdom.

I Thought It Was Just Me: Women Reclaiming Power and Courage in a Culture of Shame by Brené Brown

The world-renowned researcher and author of more than half a dozen books shares her ideas and philosophies about shame, vulnerability, and women. In these pages, Brown encourages readers to get to know—and love—their imperfections and vulnerabilities, and to share them with the world.

The Secret by Rhonda Byrne

Released in 2006, *The Secret* became a bestseller and a major influence in the lives of many who read it. The book explores the idea of the law of attraction, which purports that by thinking of what we want or need, we can influence events in the world around us. The book suggests that The Secret can be applied to all aspects of life.

A Course in Miracles Made Easy by Alan Cohen

Author Alan Cohen was a student of the original *Course in Miracles*. Here, he takes the book's core messages and distills them into their most essential nature. The tome includes teachings on love, forgiveness, and inner peace.

The Wisdom and Teachings of Stephen Covey

Author of the hugely influential book, *The 7 Habits of Highly Successful People*, Stephen Covey died in 2012, leaving behind a legacy of rich ideas and practices. Here, his teachings on things like leadership and time management are collected for readers to enjoy.

The All or Nothing Marriage by Eli J. Finkel

As marriage has evolved into its modern iteration, so too have the best practices surrounding it. Here, social psychologist Eli J. Finkel reveals the secrets to making marriage work, and to allowing each person to grow and evolve within them.

How to See Yourself As You Are by Tenzin Gyatso, the 14th Dalai Lama

His Holiness the Dalai Lama asserts in this book that all human beings can achieve happiness and meaning in their lives through knowing themselves. The book offers teachings, exercises, and personal anecdotes to send readers on their journey.

Power vs. Force by David R. Hawkins

Equating power with positive attributes such as love and courage, and force with negative attributes such as violence and anger, psychiatrist David R. Hawkins examines how humans can move toward fulfilling their potential.

Think on These Things by Krishnamurti

Through this collection of talks and essays, the late philosopher and spiritual leader Krishnamurti offers his thoughts on the state of modern personhood and all its attendant concerns. Topics include education, caring for the earth, fear, respect, and joy.

Bird by Bird by Anne Lamott

This writing craft book may seem to be about how to put words to the page, but its wisdom runs much deeper than that. Author Anne Lamott shows readers how to be patient, how to break down daunting tasks, and how to keep going in the face of challenges, one step at a time—bird by bird.

Broken Open by Elizabeth Lesser

Sometimes, the most difficult periods of our lives turn out to be the most important. That's what author Elizabeth Lesser discovered after a few years of near-constant change and upheaval. The resulting book teaches readers how to embrace change, and see that everyone around us is going through the exact same things—that we're all in this together.

Fear: Essential Wisdom for Getting Through the Storm by Thich Nhat Hahn

In this classic guide, Zen master and spiritual leader Thich Nhat Hahn offers his guidance on examining, moving through, and overcoming fear. The book includes paths to excavating the sources of our fear and facing them head-on.

Teachings on Love by Thich Nhat Hanh

This guide to loving well in all relationships—including our relationship with ourselves—draws on teachings from the Buddha's way of life as well as personal experiences and anecdotes. Thich Nhat Hanh shows readers how to use mindfulness and awareness to love one another better.

The Four Agreements by Don Miguel Ruiz

Spiritual leader and thinker Don Miguel Ruiz outlines four of the core messages present in Toltec teachings. He examines how the ways in which we relate to ourselves, and how we hold ourselves accountable in the world, are the key to a happy and successful life.

The Leader Who Had No Title by Robin Sharma

Canadian author Robin Sharma unveils his tried and true methods towards innovation, influence, recognizing opportunities, and more in this how-to guide. A sought-after speaker, Sharma's methods had previously only been available to a select few.

Future Shock by Alvin Tofler

Published in 1970, futurist Alvin Tofler explored the human, psychological effects of rapid societal change. The title came from an article Tofler had written five years prior which investigated the whiplash experienced by the average person when a lot of change—mostly technological—happens in a short period of time.

Alone Together by Sherry Turkle

In this groundbreaking exploration, MIT researcher Sherry Turkle examines how technology has given us the illusion that we are connected when in fact we're more alone than ever. The work is based on hundreds of interviews, and while Turkle found many disturbing trends in the course of her research, she also found something unexpected: hope.

Ideas by Peter Watson

In this examination of the history of ideas, Peter Watson traces original thinking back to over a million years ago, then takes readers on a journey through the eras—from the Ancient Greeks to the Renaissance to Darwinism to the internet. In doing so, he thoughtfully explores how ideas have shaped our culture and our lives.

A Return to Love by Marianne Williamson

A rumination on *A Course in Miracles* by Helen Schucman, *A Return to Love* details the author's journey towards inner peace through the acceptance of love. The book examines such concepts as having a relationship with a higher power, forgiveness, unhappiness, and fear.

Appendix III

Getting To Know Yourself: Psychometric and Personality Assessments

In previous chapters, we've emphasized how important self-knowledge can be a foundation for integrity and personal growth. To find the drive to remove our limiting beliefs and live authentically, we must know our own strengths and unique abilities. When trying to determine our own unique strengths, the assessments below can provide helpful guidance.

While no single assessment can fully capture the complexity of who we are, each can provide valuable insights into certain aspects of ourselves, allowing us to leverage our innate gifts instead of resisting or compartmentalizing them.

Kolbe Index

The Kolbe Index is a unique assessment as it does not measure intelligence, personality, or social style. Instead, it measures the instinctive ways that we take action when we strive, distributing our scores across four distinct categories so we can clearly see which of our tendencies are most dominant.

With the results of the Kolbe Index, we can gain a better sense of our own unique modus operandi (MO)—the way we like to do things in the world when we're acting fully as ourselves.

To take the KOLBE A Index, please visit:
https://secure.kolbe.com

Myers-Briggs Type Indicator (MBTI)

There are many online sources to perform the widely used MBTI self-assessment. This tool was originally developed to help individuals select occupations well suited to their personality types. Today, the test is used to help individuals understand their own personalities, including their likes, dislikes, strengths, weaknesses, possible career preferences, and compatibility with other people.[1]

To take the Myers-Briggs Type Indicator (MBTI), please visit:
https://www.themyersbriggs.com

Plum

Plum is a powerful job assessment platform designed to help individuals craft a career path that aligns with their talents and unique abilities. Combining a human-centric approach with

---

1. Ohwovoriole, T. (2024, August 27). *Which personality types are most and least compatible?*. Verywell Mind. https://www.verywellmind.com/personality-types-compatibility-8686793.

comprehensive data analytics, the platform helps generate career suggestions that are, on average, four times more accurate than competing tools.

To take Plum's career assessments, please visit:
https://www.plum.io

StrengthsFinder

The StrengthsFinder assessment, which has since been renamed the CliftonStrengths assessment, was developed by Don Clifton, a crucial figure in the field of positive psychology. The assessment is designed to identify an individual's talents and "naturally recurring [patterns] of thought, feeling, or behavior." In turn, this information allows them to invest more time into developing skills that could turn these talents into core strengths.

To take the StrengthsFinder assessment, please visit:
https://www.gallup.com/cliftonstrengths

Author's Note

The lessons in this book are the creed I live by—not usually, but always.

I believe in my heart that anyone who will make the effort to define their life in this manner and *live by it*—without bullshitting themselves, but by facing the hard truths of their own being—can reach anything they aspire to.

Start off each day with what you can do for others within the framework set forth in the book, and you will prosper.

I am excited most days by the potential I see in life, both in myself and others, and I put forth the effort to see that potential developed. If we all did the same, the world could become a much better place.

My mission in life is to give a hand to those who feel the same but need a hand in developing the tools that can help lead them down that path.

The path I reference is the sum of the parts of this book, namely goals, tenacity, values, integrity and, most of all, generosity of spirit: being willing to help in whatever way we can help the most.

—Garnet Morris, 2024

About the Authors

Olivia Chadwick, MSc in Kinesiology, is a mental performance coach, certified exercise physiologist, podcaster, speaker, and founder of Movement Medicine—a groundbreaking coaching practice featuring an integrated team of world-class leaders in exercise science. She is the host of *She Knew Better*, a podcast dedicated to showcasing guests who offer expert and compassionate advice to help us overcome life's challenges, navigate mistakes and setbacks, and elevate our potential. Chadwick resides in Saskatoon, Saskatchewan, Canada. *17 Runs* is her first book.

Garnet Morris is an entrepreneur with over 40 years of experience in the insurance industry. With only a high school education, he founded The Targeted Strategies Group (TTSG), the premier Canadian brokerage firm dedicated to helping entrepreneurs and their families protect, preserve, and optimize their net worth through life insurance policies. At the age of 40, he transformed his health by losing 130 pounds, after which he became passionate about personal fitness, self-development, and lifelong learning. Morris was born and raised in small towns in Saskatchewan and currently resides in Vancouver, British Columbia. *17 Runs* is his first book.

For more information about Olivia Chadwick and Garnet Morris, please scan the QR code below:

About the Publisher

Legacy Launch Pad is a boutique publishing company that works with entrepreneurs from all over the world. For more information about Legacy Launch Pad Publishing, go to:

www.legacylaunchpadpub.com